Fishing for Wild Trout in Scottish Lochs

Fishing for Wild Trout in Scottish Lochs

Lesley Crawford

SWAN·HILL
PRESS

First published in the UK in 1996
by Swan Hill Press, an imprint of Airlife Publishing Ltd

British Library Cataloguing in Publication Data
A catalogue record for this book
is available from the British Library

ISBN 1 85310 595 3

All photography by Lesley Crawford unless otherwise stated.

Typeset by Hewer Text Composition Services, Edinburgh
Printed in England by Butler & Tanner Ltd, Frome and London.

Swan Hill Press
an imprint of Airlife Publishing Ltd
101 Longden Road, Shrewsbury SY3 9EB

Dedication

To my sons, Andrew and Ewan, a fine brace.

Acknowledgements

I gratefully acknowledge the following for their invaluable help and assistance:

Dr R. W. Crawford BSc PhD Cchem MRSC for his advice on technical and scientific matters (as well as being there in times of crisis); Graham Brooks of Harpers Tackle Shop, Thurso for advice on tackle; Bob Brightman, Stan Clementsmith, Harry Davidson, Billy Faulkner, John Hamilton, Drew Jamieson, Douglas Kyle, Alan Porteous, Bill Rintoul, Matt Walker and Jane Wright for tactical advice for various regional waters; Jimmy Gunn of Reay for loans of rare historical books and help with Gaelic translations.

Contents

Introduction

There is something so captivating about wild trout fishing on Scotland's lochs that I can never fully describe it. It is the constant pitting of wits against the moods of a wild and elusive fish; it is listening to waves tumble onshore as the last strands of light flit over the loch at dusk; it is that last-ditch effort with a tattered old Invicta to produce the only trout of an arduous day; it is the adrenalin surge of the unexpected contrasted with that wonderful tranquillity of dancing waters; it is battling with elements that can choose at whim whether to bludgeon you with gales or caress you with silence. Wild trout fishing is all of these things and more, but I suppose the fundamental attraction of the sport is its ability to ceaselessly offer something new and exciting to learn. It is a multi-faceted recreation to be pursued on the lightest or very deepest of levels, and that makes it very special.

It is my intention to convey through the pages of this book some of wild trout loch fishing's complex attractions from knowledge which has been built up through many years of trial and error, and I will try always to strike a balance between theory and enjoyable practice. We will look at the development of Scottish loch trout angling, its ecology and the loch trout's present situation and provide you with an in-depth picture of angling for this enigmatic fish: how to do it, where and when, with much encouraging practical advice on the traditional techniques used to catch him. I would emphasise that this is not a book to read if you want to know about fishing for rainbow trout in a concrete bowl next to a motorway. Neither is it a book written from scant background knowledge – a holiday here, a visit there, a sniff of Highland air and a Walter Scott lyric on the lips. No, it concerns Scotland's wildest of wild brown trout, angling thrills and spills, warts and all. While occasionally taking a strong and critical look at today's loch fishing it also seeks to point a number of positive ways forward.

The crash and plunge of an angry trout as he fights you tooth and nail on the lonely shore of a remote hill loch is an excitement few anglers will deny is elemental and awe-inspiring. As we approach the next century more and more fishers are turning to the superb challenges of Scotland's wild trout seeking out something which will supply them with a complete contrast to their stocked 'city' fish. It was in the light of this expanding demand that this book was written, and it is aimed as much at those who already love and enjoy their wild brown trout angling as it is at the visitor or beginner trying it for the first time. My country is home to some of the finest wild brown trout fishing in Britain so let me take you now through some of the indigenous trout's long and fascinating past, show you some secrets in successfully fishing for him and above all, let me inspire you to conserve and protect this most dashing of fish for future generations.

Lesley Crawford

To me there is
no pleasure
in fishing
in anger
in greed
or in haste
LCC

1
The Scottish Tradition

Don't brood on what's past, but never forget it either

THOMAS H. RADDALL

Trout of Yore

Scotland is home to some of the purest waters in Britain and from the air appears bedecked with sparkling lochs and lochans of all shapes, depths and sizes, some 35,000 waters in total. The loch systems are spread over the length and breadth of this beautiful country and are mainly clean, well oxygenated waters fed from fast-flowing hill burns, underground springs, rainwater, rivers and rivulets. Though some lochs are considerably more fertile than others, in general, they form the ideal habitat for wild brown trout, so it is little wonder they have long been recognised as one of the most favoured destinations for the game angler. The choice of waters is bewildering, exciting and inspirational all at once and though today we see the centres for wild trout fishing being pushed further north as more 'rainbow' fisheries proliferate in central Scotland, there is still an abundance of wild trout fishing to enjoy.

The indigenous trout of our freshwater lochs are thought to have been present from around the end of the last Ice Age. Scientific investigation has shown them to be among the original fish colonisers of Scotland like the eel, salmon, stickleback, lamprey and charr. One school of thought suggests that brown trout are simply landlocked sea trout left behind when the great ice retreated and going on to flourish in freshwater as opposed to the ocean. Whatever their exact origin many early historical records dating back as far as the 1600s and 1700s, refer to 'Trouts and Falmon [salmon]' abounding in Scotland's lochs, rivers and burns. All game fish were then extremely plentiful, indeed salmon was considered the staple diet of the poor at one time and trout and charr were unceremoniously netted out of lochs to supply food for the local population.

Scotland seemed positively over endowed with wild trout according to early writings and when the Victorian predilection for hunting, fishing and shooting took off, brownies were to come in for some serious attention. Not only did the early anglers fish zealously for trout with rod and line along with less savoury methods including nets, gunpowder and an ugly technique called 'burning the water', they also took a great interest in all forms of fish breeding and massive wild trout restocking programmes were undertaken in all areas of Scotland. By the time the Marquess of Granby wrote his authoritative tome *The Trout* (1890), the Victorians had taken it upon themselves rightly or wrongly, to restock many brown trout fisheries throughout England and Scotland, thus altering for ever the true numbers of indigenous brown trout populations. It seemed the practical theories for fishery management on sporting waters in the late 1800s and early 1900s focused on pouring more and more fish into a water whether its natural spawning was self-sustaining or not. Unusual strains of trout cropped up in unexpected places such as Fife-bred 'Loch Leven' trout emanating from hill lochs in remote Sutherland or the island of Skye. Trout were transported around Scotland from loch to loch which has led to some interesting theories of origin being propounded. For example it is said that the silvery trout of Loch Katrine in the Trossachs come originally from Loch Watten in Caithness, equally I have heard it said locally that a considerable amount of the trout used to restock Caithness waters came originally from Loch Katrine!

Most anglers would see any restocking as a 'plus', but as the new introduced stock went on to breed with the native trout stocks it is possible that some unique characteristics of indigenous fish found only in specific lochs, were considerably adulterated and lost forever. Loss of a particular genetic strain of trout may not be viewed as overly important by some, however, I personally feel that in future trout conservation, recognition and preservation of any remaining isolated strains are vital in achieving proper

The magnificent Loch Leven strain of wild trout, black asterix spots and silver flanks.

status for the Scottish brown trout. Perhaps I am too much the avid natural historian but I do feel rather strongly on this matter, I like my fish as much as anything to have a sense of nationality and place.

'New blood is always a good tonic for a human being or a trouting loch,' wrote William Robertson MD in his book *Angling Resorts of Scotland* (1935) and that about summed up the theory of the late Victorian and Edwardian era. At one time nearly every body of water larger than a hectare was stocked with brown trout, albeit usually reared locally in estate hatcheries that were considerably more numerous than today. Anglers frequenting the popular fishing hotels and estates of that period seemed to demand hefty baskets for their stay; bags of fifty to seventy trout per rod per day have been recorded as unremarkable, and loch owners must have felt compelled to keep fish numbers on the high side so that guests could enjoy what they saw as 'good sport'. In general fishing hotel registers and/or game estate records show much more restocking taking place in the late nineteenth and early twentieth centuries than today. Where no localised hatchery existed it was often the practice either to net out burn trout and transplant them from streams to lochs, or to move trout from an overstocked water to one less well endowed. This kind of work was usually done by the local estates or angling associations. Unfortunately today there are much stricter legal controls governing the movement of fish, wild trout amongst them, and restocking practices such as the netting of burn trout, are difficult to do without encountering considerable legal red tape.

Throughout Caithness and Sutherland, counties today considered home to the wildest of wild fish, widespread restocking was undertaken using the services of local estate hatcheries which grew young non-migratory fish as well as migratory fish like salmon and sea trout. There was a major wild brown trout hatchery at Ardgay on the east coast of Sutherland, run by the McNicol brothers, members of a famed Sutherland gamekeeping family, up until the 1960s, when it became too uneconomic to continue on such a large scale. This hatchery was an elaborate all-year undertaking with a dozen or so stone tanks for grading and holding fish of different size and age. The hatchery covered well over an acre of land and used running water diverted from the nearby burn to flush through a graduation of smaller and larger tanks running right down to the edge of the sea. When the brothers received an order for fish they took the required number from the main system and isolated them in what were called 'starving tanks' for two days so that the water the fish were to be transported in did not become fetid with excreta. This went some way to lessen the number of mortalities usually caused when young fish were transported long distances without the aid of oxygen tanks and other modern paraphernalia. Using first a horse and cart and later a rumbling lorry they took trout out to even the most remote lochs for restocking and their skills in fish rearing and fishery

Loch Watten, Caithness.

management using very basic equipment put some more modern methods to shame.

I have had the pleasure of fishing a number of the lochs which were restocked with McNicol fish and I can safely say their efforts were quite remarkable. On one particular loch near Melvich, Sutherland, restocked several times in the past, a typical basket of spirited wild brownies will contain a deep gold-bellied strain, silvery-sided trout, a trout with large black circular markings and the more usual common black and red spotted trout. Although there is no way of knowing which is the original genetic strain for that loch, it is heartening to see that all the fish, no matter their coloration, are in fine and thriving condition, the direct descendants of trout placed there so long ago. So it would seem that while we cast a fly for our wild trout many of these fish are the progeny of naturalised 'stocked' browns put there over the past century. However, I would state quite categorically that this in no way detracts from their superb fighting abilities which are revered by sportsmen the world over.

The Victorians also gave a great number of exotic classifications to the humble brown trout but on a point of coloration and markings it is interesting to note that in the *Statistical Account of Scotland 1791* there are numerous references to 'large red trouts' existing in various lochs in Sutherland and descriptions of wild trout as 'red trout' crop up frequently in other writings of that period. Quite how the red trout became the 'brownie' we know and love today is not clear; it may have had something to do with the red flesh indicative of good quality crustacean-feeding fish, whereas 'brown trout' is more descriptive of its exterior markings. There also seems to be further confusion of trout with the, then more plentiful, Arctic charr, also known as 'red bellies' (Gaelic, *tar deargan** or *tarragan*) in lochs. This deepwater fish does closely resemble the common trout in shape and size though its colours tend toward red and green with golden fins and underbelly. In days past they were netted in October when they came in to spawn at the shallow edges of such well-known Highland lochs as Loch Loyal or Loch Borralie in north Sutherland. When engaged in spawning the charr were highly vulnerable and made an easy catch, but the fish did provide an important source of food for the local population. 'Red' trout or 'brown', wild or hatchery-reared, the quality of the Scottish wild trout is unsurpassed and it has been greatly revered by sportsmen since the very earliest accounts of loch-style angling.

Some Pioneers of Loch Fishing

Scotland as a nation has fostered generations of wild brown trout anglers and this is where most modern-day 'loch-style' angling has its deepest roots. A huge tradition of trout loch fishing has evolved, stretching back over centuries and it is important to recognise the depth of this history for it gives the contemporary picture its true perspective. Today, because many of Scotland's waters are still relatively isolated, the visiting angler may well feel he is the first to cast a fly or drift in a boat on a remote high loch and quite rightly so, for one of their principal attractions is indeed their solitude. However, in days past someone, somewhere, will almost certainly have been there before him. It may not have been yesterday, in that season or even in the last decade but an angler *will* have been there at some time. Modern wild trout fishers follow in the footsteps of some giants of angling history and it is perhaps indicative of the sport's past popularity that a heavyweight *Sportsman's and Tourist's Guide to Scotland* was published monthly rather than yearly during the latter part of the 1800s when the Victorian 'hunting, shooting and fishing' era was in full swing.

These 'paperback' books, often several centimetres thick, were published from Edinburgh and edited by a redoubtable gentleman, Mr Watson Lyall. They went into the most comprehensive detail imaginable on all matters pertaining to game pursuits; who owned what, who leased what, the quality of fishings and shootings available including average weights or bags, where to stay and how to obtain permission to fish, *ad infinitum*! Great lists like this may sound dry but these *Sportsman's Guides* make compelling

* Note the Gaelic *tar* for charr. I strongly suspect that as with many phonetic spellings of Gaelic names and places which occurred in the past, 'charr' or 'char' is merely an English corruption of the true Gaelic name.

reading representing probably the most comprehensive early records available on trout fishing throughout Scotland.

Looking through them it is possible to see history come alive and in one edition written in 1875 by Watson Lyall, there are pertinent references to my own home village of Reay on the Caithness and Sutherland border. Lyall alludes to fishing being available on Lochs Calam (Calvin), Na Scirach (Saorach) and Thormand (Thormaid) out from the 'Old Inn' at Reay. Our modern home is a neighbouring house to this lovely old building and by strange coincidence history repeated itself over 100 years later when I partnered a lease on the last of the aforementioned lochs selling a limited number of visiting permits to anglers. I felt inordinately proud to be able to follow almost exactly in the path of some tremendous anglers of old, except I have a motor car and iron road to get there unlike my forebears who were conveyed by pony and trap along a dirt track and endured a lengthy tramp over the boggy moor to the lochs. Admittedly Lyall's Victorian *Sportsman's Guides* do suffer from reporting anglers occasionally exaggerating or distorting catches to the favour or detriment of certain areas and there are some very strange misinterpretations and spellings of Gaelic names, many being recorded phonetically (see Appendix II Translations of Gaelic Loch Names). However, despite this, they clearly show Scotland's loch trout fishing as a traditional and extremely popular pursuit with its origins firmly set down in the sporting past.

Numerous fine anglers came on the scene at the end of the last century and in the early 1900s. Their names are legion but Stoddart, St John, Colquhoun, Malloch and R. C. Bridgett spring readily to mind, and it is from their method and style that our modern loch-style tactics have developed. Though there are much earlier works on the general techniques of British trout fishing particularly on rivers, one of the first to mention Scottish loch-style fishing is W. C. Stewart's book *The Practical Angler*, first published in 1857, but updated and revised no less than fifteen times up to the 1940s. Though Stewart did not appear to rate loch fishing particularly highly compared with river technique he does summarise well the approach required for wild trout lochs. Strangely, in much of the angling writing of the Victorian period and to a lesser extent now, loch trout fishing nearly always appears to be rated a poor second cousin to river trout fishing and there appears to be no attempt or wish to correlate the two techniques required. Historically, river trout fishing was *the* thing and lochs were viewed as an easier, softer angling alternative, requiring considerably less skill and ability. I find this rather odd for brown trout found in lochs will feed avidly on the same things as river trout; they behave in a similar cautious and elusive way; anatomically they are identical reproducing at similar times of year in virtually identical environmental conditions; and frankly, in dour circumstances, they are both just as difficult to attract!

Stewart himself accidentally contradicts the dim view placed on loch fishing by pointing out that any river technique may be used on lochs with success. It seemed to be the 'tiresome monotony' of fishing in still water which irked him more, that and the apparent disbelief that the quality of a loch could be analysed from its shores. Bank anglers 'can never tell with any certainty which is a good bay and which a bad one', he stated, something I am afraid I will dispute further in this book in the chapter 'A Contrast of Lochs' which discusses, amongst other things, how to assess the potential of a loch from its shores! His categorising of loch fishing as less exacting also seems to stem from the use in the old days of a loch boatman who would naturally do all the work in guiding the angler to the appropriate best fishing area, put on the correct fly and let his charge do the rest. Today very few Scottish loch anglers have their own boatman so that source of local knowledge has gone and anglers are left entirely to their own devices. For all that, Stewart's general advice on trout fishing techniques is highly practical and just as relevant today as it was then.

The rare book *Scotch Loch Fishing* written in 1882 by the mysteriously named 'Black Palmer' is a delight. Obviously the classing of loch fishing as a poor second to river angling during that era gave Black Palmer some concern for he picks up on prevailing opinion in his introduction, making considerable effort to dispel the myth that the abilities required in loch fishing are inferior. He then details the various techniques involved and describes the tackle used for loch fishing as a rod of not less than 4.2m (14ft)

Preparing for the day ahead, Loch Caladail, Sutherland.

and where sea trout were likely to be present, a rod of 4.8m (16ft) was the norm. Since at that time the rod was likely to have been made of heavy greenheart or hickory, large biceps must also have been obligatory! Flies he describes as tied to 'Loch Leven size' are the March Brown, Harelugs, Zulu and Red Spider varieties along with a number tied with mallard wings. 'Black Palmer' advises fishing with at least three flies paying particular attention to working the bob fly from the boat and casting a short controllable line. 'When you raise a fish strike at once,' he adds, which shows brown trout were just as quicksilver then as they are now. There is a lovely chapter in this book about what to do after a day's fishing. 'The angler should always have a sound dinner after a day's fishing and a glass of whisky, or even two,' Black Palmer advises, and 'your fishing bag should be washed out and hung up to dry by the servants of the house' – why are my family not following the good man's guidance today one wonders?

Somewhat of an unjustified aversion toward loch-style fishing continued through historical writings with many leading angling writers simply dismissing loch trouting when comparing it to other methods of fly fishing, particularly river trouting. Happily the book *Loch Fishing* (*c*.1924) by R. C. Bridgett squarely set the record straight. Bridgett was a highly respected 'thinking angler' far ahead of his time and his innovative writings on the natural history of loch trout and tactics to catch him as well as imitative fishing, fly-tying and entomology were exceptionally advanced for the period. Most of his theories still work very well today and if there is one historical book to refer to, both for good reading and comprehensive analysis of everything to do with loch trouting, this is it. Get a copy while you still can for they are becoming more and more difficult to obtain.

During the mid-1930s loch angling seemed to be written about far less often than river trouting, perhaps because stocks of river trout were more plentiful and relatively easily accessible when compared with the vastness of Scottish loch systems many of which are centred in remote and rarely visited areas. Travel, particularly to some of the better but more isolated lochs, was a long and arduous undertaking (some would argue it still is!) and consequently there was a dearth of comprehensive knowledge on wild trout loch fishing apart from one or two notable exceptions. The further north you went the more minimal the road systems, though the rail network did compensate for some of these difficulties and it took a particularly determined type of angler to tour in the northernmost half of the country in the war years. Even then they did not always meet with the required success to repay their exhausting efforts in reaching their destinations. William Robertson bemoans long tiresome walks in the Highlands for what he saw as a 'few dour fish' and he soundly berates hoteliers for not restocking their lochs!

'For sheer sport I reckon a really rough day with numerous squalls on a wild and desolate Highland loch surrounded by frowning mountains cannot be beaten'. McDonald Robertson, circa 1930.

However, just as some saw the remoteness of the Highlands as an angling disadvantage, others revelled in it. McDonald Robertson of Edinburgh wrote several books on game fishing during the 1930 to 1950 period and recounted with great verve his visits to wild and remote trout lochs. He wrote in the 'derring-do' style of his Victorian predecessors and this was to make him one of the most read angling raconteurs of that time. Even the look of the man with his tailored kilt, neatly pressed white shirt and 'brillcreamed' locks smacks of a bygone age when 'gentlemen and their gillies' made the Highlands of Scotland their playground. 'For sheer sport I reckon a really rough day with numerous squalls on a wild and desolate Highland loch surrounded by frowning mountains cannot be beaten,' he wrote in his first book *In Scotland with a Fishing Rod* and I would echo such sentiments wholeheartedly. He muses on a trio of waters in Berwickshire where he says the trout grew to 'tremendous size' because of the occasional addition of grass cuttings to the lochs and speculated that this increased growth had occurred because they had fed on insects emanating from the decaying vegetation. There may be some truth in this as there are other accounts of hay bales having been placed in lochs in the hope of assisting feeding for the trout. A later book by McDonald Robertson *Wade the River Drift the Loch* gets more into the real nitty-gritty on how to fish trout lochs around 1948. His advice is basic yet practical and he proffers the following: 'The great secret of loch fishing is not to be discouraged. Keep on casting and try to keep the flies in the water as much as possible.' Things do not change much do they? Philip Gunn also contributed a very short chapter to this book and his counsel is adroit on loch fishing when he points out that anglers, perhaps more versed in river fishing, should not believe wild loch trout to be fish which 'impatiently await the angler's flies'. He quite rightly corrects this thinking by stating that even waters seldom fished may be wild and dour and that 'one may fish for hours on a surface unbroken by a rise'. In such circumstances he favoured changing flies periodically and when using three flies having a Butcher or Peter Ross along with a nymph pattern. This tactic is still much favoured today when loch fishing may demand a change of fly perhaps every fifteen minutes.

A delightful little book *How to Catch Trout* by 'Three Anglers' (for some reason the book was written anonymously), originally published in 1888 but revised in 1943 , devotes ten pages to how to fish for loch trout but the chapter's first words begin, 'Although loch fishing does not require the same amount of skill as river fishing, it is still a most enjoyable pastime, the great attraction being the superior size of trout caught.' I wonder if W. C. Stewart played an anonymous part in composing its original editions! However, apart from taking the by now standard sideswipe at loch fishing, the book is helpful enough and we can see a considerable amount of today's accepted techniques emerging from its pages. Rods recommended for use by the authors were still greenheart but split cane and bamboo had also made an appearance. There were no synthetic nylon leaders available then and 'gut' casts were often made from sheep's intestines. These were a fragile affair which, if allowed to dry out, frequently became brittle and broke unless stored wet in cast wallets usually made of leather with a spongy damp interior. Casts were some- times soaked in tea to discolour the glitter, a clever move not commonly in use today when our synthetic substances are not thought to need it. Fly lines were of waterproofed silk or silk and horse hair woven together and flies favoured were often tied on double hooks, usually referred to as 'Wee Doubles' or 'Leven Flies'. Famous anglers of that period selected loch trout flies quite similar to our own loch-style patterns, for example P. D. Malloch (of the Perth tackle shop still in business under this name) listed his flies which he called quaintly 'P. D. Malloch's Choice of Loch Leven "Powerful Killers" as 'Grouse and Claret, Butcher, Blae and Black, Wickham's Fancy, Greenwell's Glory' and so on and they took pride of place in any expert's box. All these dressings are still much in demand today; less commonly seen are other trout flies of that period such as the Professor, the Bloody Doctor, the Moderator and the Col. Downman, all presumably named after their creators.

Before we leave the pioneers of old there is one other angling raconteur I must mention with the grand title of V. Carron Wellington who seems to have fished extensively all around Scotland with the redoubtable McDonald Robertson. In 1952 he wrote *The Adventures of a Sporting Angler* and though this is probably one of the most floridly written books on angling I have ever come across, it does capture the imagination in a way few more modern writers can emulate. Ignoring the twee prose there are some remarkable angling tales of Wellington engaging on walks of ten miles or so just to reach a particular loch whereupon, should he not be able to cast far enough, he would simply undress, clench the rod in his teeth and swim out to the nearest island or promontory. If he secured trout he would then string them to his belt on curtain hooks, swim back over the loch and then squelch home in the same soaking boots and shorts! He also fished for trout in some frankly extraordinary places as for example when he walked along the base of the Corrie Halloch (Shalloch) gorge near Braemore, Wester Ross, to fish in the dark pools below the remote Falls of Measach. This he managed without modern climbing harnesses and was even able to catch some fish, though they were very ugly and black. Some of his escapades were downright dangerous as when he accidentally disturbed a pair of nesting swans whilst swimming across a stretch of open water in a loch and they turned on him making a violent attack with their great wings quite determined to beat him senseless, or equally hair-raising, the time he almost drowned alone in an isolated loch near Lochinver after he became entangled in treacherous lily beds whilst wading along the shore. Had it not been somewhat spoiled by gushing descriptions this book could have become perhaps a standard work on the unique excitement of fishing for the wild trout in secret lonely glens; as it is, it is usually confined to a dusty library shelf, a pity.

From simple practicalities to tales of 'derring-do' we can always learn much from the perspective of what has gone before. Though these pioneers with all their eccentricities, skills and foibles have long since gone to that great loch in the sky their exploits live on, helping to enrich the traditional techniques of trout loch angling within Scotland.

2

Scotland's Loch Trout Fishing in the 1990s

Do not seek to follow in the footsteps of the men of old; seek what they sought.

MATSUO BASHO

Wild Browns and Rainbows

In Scotland today you are going to meet with a vast choice of waters, some containing entirely wild game fish like the trout, the sea trout and/or the salmon; some with mixtures of brown trout and coarse fish populations; some with stocked browns and rainbow trout; and some exclusively stocked with rainbows. Perhaps one of the most significant influences our angling forebears were to have on our wild trout fishing was their insistence on continual restocking of lochs for, as general fish culture techniques advanced, the brown trout in Scotland found disfavour with its 'farmers' who chose instead the easier controlled, more resilient and faster growing American rainbow. From about the 1960s we see both a significant downturn in brown trout rearing, said by many to have become too difficult a job for too little reward, and a subsequent upswing in rainbow trout fishery popularity. Spurred on perhaps by the success of rainbow trout fisheries across the border and also by their customers' demands for more and bigger fish, Scottish trout breeders took to rearing rainbows with a vengeance. From around the mid-1960s onward there was an upswing in reservoir 'still-water' angling and the rainbow trout presented the fishery manager with an attractive money-making venture few could ignore. As a rapacious feeder it could be far quicker 'grown on' to present the angler with a hefty specimen thereby covering him and more importantly the fishery, in glory. Rainbow trout generally seemed capable of fulfilling most anglers' dreams and their increased favour coincided with a slow spiral of decline on many wild trout fisheries when a number of very large game estates containing prime trout fishing became uneconomic and were sold off in smaller lots often to new owners with little or no interest in wild trout. Many of the original brown trout hatcheries closed altogether or altered their use to concentrate solely on the rearing of the more lucrative salmon or rainbow trout. In a move some would see as monetarily prudent and others would see as a shirking of responsibility, many riparian loch owners let any restocking of trout be done by the local associations rather than undertaking the work themselves. Where thriving and conscientious local associations existed, restocking and general care of wild trout has continued quite well, though in the 1990s such organisations often have to buy in trout from external sources rather than rearing their own fish.

Demand for angling, particularly near the main conurbations began increasing in the 1960s and 70s, and indeed is still growing for trout fishing is a highly rated hobby, one of the most popular sports in Britain. Faced with this burgeoning angling demand and a possible public perception that apparently there were not enough obliging wild trout left, the rainbow trout fishery came into its own, some more prudently operated than others. Though this is not a book on rainbow trout fishing let me say this of our now nationally spread non-native species. American rainbow trout which have been properly cared for and allowed to grow 'wild' in a natural fertile environment do indeed present the angler with a worthy prize and are well worth the fishing fees. However flabby specimens force-fed with pellets and grown in tanks so small the fish end up with no tails are not my idea of a 'game' fish. I do not feel that hapless beasts swimming aimlessly in circles in a murky pond where anything from sweetcorn to

Restocking was widespread in the late 1800s and early 1900s; today it is mainly undertaken by local Associations.

luncheon meat is used to catch them, can be equated with Scottish trout fishing as I know it. A number of 'fisheries' are attached to rainbow trout farms and while I feel they may allow youngsters the chance to catch a first fish, they cannot help but give a completely misleading impression of what Scottish trout fishing is all about. On a more positive note, standards of rainbow management are slowly altering for the better. With a heavy proliferation of rainbow trout fisheries in the last ten years some minimum standards and a Code of Practice have been devised by the Scottish Stillwater Fisheries Association (Appendix III). This is a welcome move for like it or not these fisheries fulfil an important need in game fishing and, for both the welfare of the fish and the angler, it is important they follow reasonable methods of management.

Where rainbows have been added into existing wild brown trout populations in freshwater lochs the effects have been mixed. In some cases the greedier, slightly less cautious American fish appears to have usurped the wild brown altogether, in others it is still possible to catch a brown and a rainbow together in the one outing. Where rainbows are introduced to compete with the indigenous browns for a poor natural food supply the brownies often become extremely hard to attract and can disappear from surface feeding altogether. However, when the two types of trout are together in a fertile water with plenty of natural food the results are variable. The Lake of Menteith is an example, for as a once 'wild' fishery it often produced good browns but then, after the addition of rainbows, the catches of browns significantly decreased in the following years. Today it is quite rare for brownies to be caught on Menteith though I am told they are still present. Recently, in the early 1990s, the principal Scottish wild brown trout water of Loch Leven (Fife), so famous it is known worldwide and has a strain of trout called after it, had short-living rainbows added to its fish population. This was in an attempt to offset the worsening catches of browns due to pollution from sewerage and agricultural practices completely altering both fishing conditions and trout behaviour. While I can see this as a practical management move to ensure the fishery still makes an income as steps are taken to redress some of the environmental damage, I do think it sad that the once traditional home of Scottish wild trout angling has now become just another 'rainbow' fishery. But then again am I just getting too old-fashionedly purist like my forebears who saw river trout fishing as somehow 'better' than loch trout fishing – who knows?

The Current Wild Choice

Leaving rainbows aside now, I have to mention them as wherever the visitor goes on the Scottish mainland today it is possible he may encounter them at some stage, I would like to paint a broad picture of where the principal areas for wild trout are as it is important to have some basic grounding in order to be able to choose wisely. There are quite a number of comprehensive local and national guidebooks available on this subject on where to fish for wild trout (see Bibliography) but you are quite safe in two basic assumptions, firstly the further north you go in Scotland the more dense the wild trout populations become and secondly the further north you travel, the less dense are the coarse fish varieties. Indeed north of Inverness there are very few coarse fish apart from some fairly isolated pike and perch populations.

Throughout my angling lifetime I have travelled the trout waters of Scotland with profound enjoyment if sometimes varying degrees of success, going through that great and wonderful learning process called fishing. As a young slip of an angler I can recall trout from Argyll hill lochs, visits to Perthshire, my father bringing home fish from the Campsie fells, Carron and Antermony and my brother also returning with strings of brownies from the River Luggie, a once lovely trout stream near our home, then owned by Sir William Whitelaw. I fondly recall family holidays near Brora in Sutherland when it took two days to get there and the trout bass seemed regularly to burst at the seams. It was here in a tiny burn that I caught my first wild brownie to the fly and was so excited I must have run half a mile to tell my parents of the conquest but on reaching them I was so out of breath only grunts and gesticulations would come out – well I was only about eight at the time! Or twenty years later when first married to a fanatical mountaineer, relishing the fishings of the big mountain ranges like those of Skye, Lochaber and Wester Ross while my husband cheerfully engaged in yomping up the nearest precipice. Island hopping was popular with us both and Mull, Orkney and Rhum were visited amongst others. The first two had great trout fishing, Orkney especially, and on Rhum I fished a small lochan below the jagged peaks of Askival, a mountain from which our present house takes its name. We left Glasgow to live in Aberdeen in the early 1980s, where river fishing began to interest me but after two years there and hardly even enough time to get on the waiting list we headed north to Reay on the border of Caithness and Sutherland, an absolute mecca for the wild trout angler. Our two sons were born here and know little else but the Highland way of life.

The broad guidance I can give you in selecting a wild trout area to visit is therefore based on many years of trial and error around the country and when you make your decisions one of the first essentials is to . . .

Decide your Priorities

Anglers resident in Scotland know it as the big expansive place it is but visitors especially from abroad look at it and say 'Ha, could fish that in a day!' I recently had a call from the States asking just whereabouts was the best trout fishing lake in 'yoh lil' country' and that he was coming for a week and could I teach him to fish on it? Needless to say I advised him to look no further than Caithness and Sutherland but he flew in to Edinburgh and I never heard any more, he's probably still on Gladhouse! Just because Scotland seems a small country do not also assume it has few waters, it is in fact covered in highly diverse freshwater lochs and to get the best from your fishing it is probably wiser to concentrate on one relatively confined area. That choice of angling district must first and foremost depend on what *you* want from your trout fishing and you really have to plan accordingly to get the most from your angling.

In deciding those angling essentials therefore, think about the kind of wild trout fishing you want, wild and remote or right by the road? What style of fishing are you looking for, lots of boat drifting or lots of wading? Do you want big, difficult, specimen fish or smaller free-rising ones or a mix of the two? How much are you prepared to spend on accommodation, travelling, etc? Accommodation prices vary from top-flight hotels to basic B & Bs with caravanning or self-catering also a possibility but travel,

Decide your priorities – boat or bank?

especially flying, can take a big chunk from your wallet before you even reach your fishing destination so budgets have to be carefully considered. And what is the likely cost of the fishing itself? Usually wild trout fishing is quite reasonably priced in Scotland and as a very rough guide you can expect to pay anything between £5 to £10 per day to bank fish and around £15–25 per day for the use of a rowing boat, engines can add more. Accessibility of wet weather alternatives for smaller companions might have to be considered, I have found that out the hard way when irate three-year-olds protest vehemently at any outing in the country which does not involve a sandy beach and blazing sunshine laid on. Children and better halfs may also want reasonable access to civilisation for shopping, cinema, swimming pool etc.; their needs have to be accounted for if you are going to get any peace to fish! If solely in the company of other like-minded adults however, the proximity of a watering hole after a hard day on the lochs might take on crucial significance. Detail your preferences and get out the nearest map of Scotland because we can usually satisfy even the most pernickety of trout anglers.

The Scottish Lochs

I cannot hope to list every wild trout loch you could visit, I would still be writing this in the year 2000, instead let me give you a whirl and a birl around most of the principal regions for brownies. If the rolling country of the Borders or Dumfries and Galloway is your penchant then look out for trout fishing in the Hawick, Selkirk, Peebles, Kelso, Newton Stewart, Castle Douglas and Stranraer areas. The lochs are not extremely numerous and a number have had to be restocked either with rainbow or browns. Some also contain high proportions of coarse fish like pike and perch and they are popular venues with those pursuing this branch of angling. The area is a great beauty spot and for those who perhaps like to combine river fishing with the loch this is a good area with its principal waters being the famed Tweed, the Teviot, the Whiteadder, the Esk, the Cree and the Nith. I think my most enduring memories of the borders apart from racing through them on that awful A74 to reach southern destinations like Liverpool or Manchester, were of family weekend breaks there, when the black smoke of 1960s austere, industrial Glasgow was left briefly behind for the leafy lane appeal of Burns country at its best.

The Strathclyde region, my old stomping ground, encompasses a huge area, some of it with excellent trout lochs and some of it pretty nondescript. Ayrshire and the Clyde valley are geographically well known to me, principally because I worked several summers near Largs, but unfortunately I was so busy pursuing my other great love – racquet sports – I paid

the fishings scant attention. However I have it on good authority that though the lochs are relatively few, some in the Kilbirnie, Ayrshire, area are worth a cast and there are also lochs near Ardrossan and Straiton. In the upper Clyde valley there are some small wild trout reservoirs including the Daer, Camps and Dunside reservoirs and, as these form part of the general water catchment area of the River Clyde, they come under the benefits of the Clyde Protection Order.

'Basically, anything north of Lenzie (near Glasgow) is worth fishing for brown trout!' so pronounced my father, an ardent trout enthusiast of the 1960s and 70s. In fact while we lived there this was quite true for the glut of rainbow trout fisheries in the central belt had not yet begun and our village, then not just an adjunct of Glasgow, was conveniently situated for a quick getaway to the lochs and rivers further north. So convenient in fact, my mother, not a fishing fan, frequently cursed its situation as dinners grew cold on tables awaiting the traveller's return. What is now known as north Strathclyde was our playground, with my father ardently fishing the lochs of Stirlingshire and the Trossachs. Places like the Carron Dam, Lochs Ard or Katrine were some of his favourites and happily they still contain brown trout. There is a little tale of his being invited to fish on the rainbow-stocked Lake of Menteith by the then owner, Lady Orr–Ewing. She provided the picnic hamper and my father the whisky and a glorious evening was had though it ended with Dad, more versed in brownie tactics, raising but then unceremoniously losing the only rainbow of the day. Oddly enough he never was invited back! A number of the lochs in this large region are now controlled by Strathclyde Regional Council and they include Loch Katrine, Loch Arklet and Glen Finglas. Aberfoyle is a good base for the lochs of Chon, Ard, Vennachar and Achray and we must not forget the 'bonny banks' of Loch Lomond. Strangely, though I visited Loch Lomond many times, sailing on it, swimming in it, casting over it and even working on its shores for a year, I rarely had much success there, inexperience of youth perhaps. It is a big windswept loch but still very beautiful, despite its hordes of 'day-trippers'.

At the time my fixation with racquet sports was at its height in the 1960s and 70s there was an intense rivalry between the cities of Glasgow and Edinburgh. Consequently as a Glaswegian, anything pleasurable like trout fishing was *verboten* for me on the east coast, one simply did not visit this area unless one was going to knock hell out of the opposition on a squash court or in a table-tennis arena! However I must not allow past differences to cloud my vision and today Lothian Regional Council have many fine and well-managed trout lochs available in the east coast area. They include Gladhouse, Glencorse, Clubbiedean, Harperrig, Crosswood and Hopes; there is also an assortment of brown trout fishing available in the West Calder and West Lothian areas. The Tweedsmuir hills hold some interesting

Scottish Ladies team captain, Nicki Coull, slogs it out in a flat calm on Loch Leven, Fife while the gillie rates the opposition.

small fisheries, again managed by Lothian Council and these number Talla, Fruid and Megget. The Council have a sound supervisory role in the welfare of their fish stocks with all anglers required to submit a detailed catch return of fish sizes caught and number returned with blanks also noted. From this information they build up a picture of the way each fishery is performing and operate a management scheme whereby some reservoirs are restocked frequently, some are rested and the surrounding area for natural recruitment in spawning streams is also monitored. Work like this is to be commended as proper sustainable management of the wild brown (see also Chapter 11).

On into the Kingdom of Fife now to what was Scotland's most famous brown trout loch of old – the great Loch Leven. Loch Leven trout have been known for centuries for their beauty and grace, silver flanked with black asterisk spots, they were every angler's dream and that is what made Loch Leven so famous – its fish. Eggs, stripped and fertilised, were transported all over the world for restocking and I have relatives in New Zealand who fish avidly for direct descendants of Leven fish! Unfortunately a range of complex factors including escalating eutrophication of the loch has resulted in brown trout catches diminishing on Leven to a shadow of their former selves and in 1993 the loch was stocked with 'stop-gap', short-living, sterile rainbows while measures were looked at to curb the extraordinary over-enrichment of this water. Leven is perhaps one of the most drastic examples of the cumulative effects of modern-day pollution, the principal villain of the piece being the element phosphorus emanating from local sewerage, agriculture and industrial waste. Over-enriching of the water has added to algal blooms which detract greatly from the fishing quality, though the overall effect on fish numbers and quality is not entirely clear as such blooms have been a feature of this loch as far back as the early 1900s prior to the heavy industrialisation and human population growth in the area. Perhaps the most drastic effect of the pollution is the complete change of fishing technique it has brought. Though the fish are still there gone are the days of light floating lines and traditional flies. Instead local anglers have to resort to heavy sinking lines and bumping rainbow lures like the Cat's Whisker along the murky bottom to catch the brown trout. – Those who would like to gain a further environmental insight into some of the extensive research which has been undertaken on Leven by bodies such as the SNH, Institute of Freshwater Ecology and others can obtain a copy of the publication *The Loch Leven Trout Fishery – its Future* from the Institute of Fisheries Management (See Appendix III). Other well-known waters in Fife, mainly stocked with brown and/or rainbow include Loch Ore, Heatheryford, Glendevon, Glenfarg and of course Loch Fitty which is exclusively rainbow.

Going north away from the central belt Argyll and Perthshire await the fly fisher's attention. Both large counties are extremely popular angling destinations and I rate them both as excellent for trout fishing and general scenic value. To begin with Argyll, always a favourite place for family holidays as a child, and now with children of my own I would have little hesitation in going back though I do find that things have altered somewhat from the 1960s and 70s. There seems to be so much more monoculture forestry now, something I do not recall from my early days. Lochs Awe and Avich are the principal big waters, now happily covered by a Protection Order and they both can provide excellent fishing. Many moons ago I visited the long finger of the Argyll peninsula which ends at the dramatic Mull of Kintyre. We fished a few remote lochs like Tangy and Lussa taking small, but spirited, browns and they are apparently still present in the lochs today. There is a big conglomeration of trout lochs around the Oban, Kilmelford and Lochgilphead areas and I have fished these much more recently with varying amounts of fortune. They contain good quality browns and one or two have sea trout occasionally within their depths. Some involve a lengthy tramp into hills but the walking is not particularly rough and the scenery attractively rolling and soft. The outlying islands of Argyll include Mull, Islay, Gigha and Jura and they have a small number of good lochs available. The first two have excellent waters and in addition Islay has a reputation for fine malt whisky but that is another tale! Gigha is a tiny island with one loch but it is worth visiting to view its extraordinary aquamarine, clear seas over white sands, quite magnificent in sunshine. Jura has some striking hills on it known as the Paps of Jura and there are one or two lochs on its western seaboard. Perhaps the most attractive thing about fishing anywhere in Argyll is its proximity to an attractive sea coastline. I recall walking back over the hills from a loch above Kilmelford to quite the most glorious sunset I have ever seen. Tiny black boats bobbed and swayed in silhouette as golden ripples of sea danced to a standstill in the little harbour – lovely memories and some lovely trout.

If most of Argyll is fronted by seas most of Perthshire is landlocked until it becomes absorbed into its grander title of 'Tayside', which encompasses the seaboard towns of Dundee, Arbroath and Montrose. This is still one of our own most popular holiday destinations and its fishings are dominated by the mighty River Tay water system. There are some immense hills dominating this area and the fishing can be very spectacular in the Rannoch and Crianlarich areas. There are also fine trout lochs in the Tummel, Pitlochry, Aberfeldy, Dunkeld, Killin and Blair Atholl districts. Loch Tay is vast and a bit daunting but if you get local advice and/or a gillie it is worth fishing usually by boat, and salmon are also present. Further east there are good fishings at Blairgowrie, Kirriemuir and at Forfar and fishing out from the Dundee area are the Lintrathen, Monikie and Crombie waters. The fishings are all what I would call quite 'civilised', that is you can fish all day in grand quite remote scenery but return at the day's end to a well-serviced centre, and cities like Perth or Dundee with swimming pools and leisure centres are great for kids too!

The Grampian area, despite its size, is not over endowed with trout lochs, in fact they are quite scarce for such a big landscape but there are some waters available for the visitor in the Braemar, Fettercairn, Forres and Elgin areas amongst others. This is a big agricultural and moorland region famed for its salmon rivers including the Spey, the Dee, Don and Deveron and of course it is a popular hill-walking area dominated by the distinguished Cairngorm massif.

Lochaber and Inverness encompass another vast mountainous region and the trout waters here increase in quality the further north you go. There are fine lochs in the Fort William, Spean Bridge, Laggan and Glen Moriston area; Lochs Lochy, Arkaig, Loyne, Cluanie, Garry and Quoich are only some of the bigger waters. The main watershed, Loch Ness and the Caledonian Canal, forms a great string of water running north-east from the 'Fort' to Inverness and note that some of the smaller, less publicised, outlying waters, are well worth a cast. For instance there is an excellent cluster of lochs on the east of Loch Ness, Lochs Ruthven and Duntelchaig are the best known, and it is a great area for wild trout, a little off the beaten track but still accessible to the major town of Inverness. Further to the west

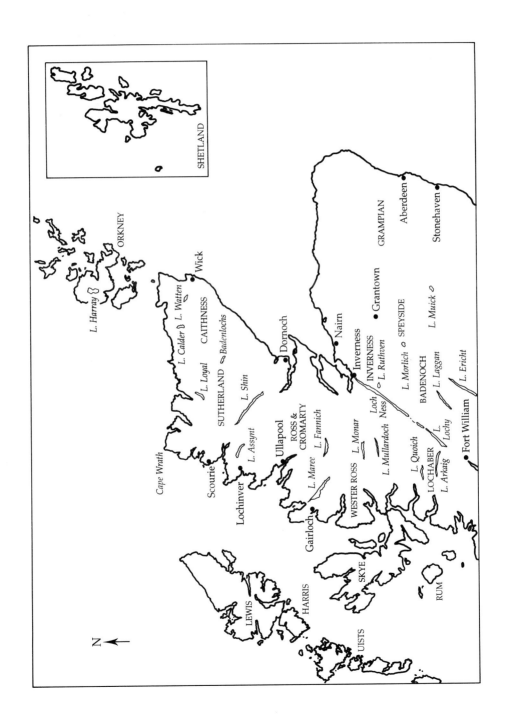

there are good lochs in the Glen Affric area, Lochs Mullardoch, Monar, Affric and Benevean being just some, and the majestic scenery makes this area worth visiting as much as the wild trout inhabiting its lochs. One thing about these big lochs is to remember to prepare yourself for some very exposed fishing, they are massive, windy places and I can still painfully remember brushing with the first stages of hypothermia on a freezing afternoon on remote Loch Monar, and it was August!

From Kyle of Lochalsh on the western seaboard you may take the ferry to Skye, though as I write a road bridge has been opened, which in my opinion, rather detracts from the romance of going 'Over the Sea to Skye'. Nevertheless this island has fantastic hills in the Black and Red Cuillin and is renowned as a mountaineering mecca. Less acknowledged but equally to be admired are its dramatic trout lochs, the principal of which lie to the north of Portree. The enigmatic Storr Lochs of Skye have brought me some of my largest brown trout from the western half of Scotland so be warned!

Easter and Wester Ross are where the fun really begins for wild trout. Going west from Dingwall the place seems covered in waters ending with some really cracking lochs around the Gairloch, Shieldaig area and north-wards toward Ullapool. Some very famous lochs lie here including Lochs Maree, Fionn, Shieldaig Lodge Hotel lochs, National Trust lochs at Poolewe and the Gairloch AC lochs. I particularly like Gairloch as it offers good family holidays and lovely sandy beaches, I have also had some hard tussles in isolated tarns around there with fast and dashing browns so go

A brace of fine wild browns from the hills.

prepared. In the Ullapool district you may fish near Leckhelm, at the Dam Lochs (a strange network of Hydro Board lochs which are stepped in dams – they had a lunar landscape appeal when I fished there in a drought); also try your luck on Loch Achall and others.

From this busy sea port you can take the ferry to the Western Isles of Lewis and Harris (Outer Hebrides) and here the wild trout fishing is quite outstanding, some of the best in Britain though the Orcadians and Shet-landers may dispute this somewhat! The Isle of Lewis has a profileration of excellent quality trout lochs dotted across its wild landscape, however, note that some of the waters also contain sea trout and salmon and are privately owned by various sporting estates. Access to some of these waters is strictly controlled and usually has to be prearranged because of the salmon interest, a policy which does not always find favour with the locals – the Outer Hebrides are hotbeds for poaching! However there are numerous brown trout lochs freely available on Lewis through the Stornaway AC, the Scaliscro Estate office and fishings are also on offer through the Loch-maddy Hotel, North Uist. South Uist and Benbecula have many excellent waters available through the Lochboisdale Hotel, Orasay Inn and the Bornish Stores amongst others. Harris has numerous water systems which interlink and many contain salmon and sea trout, for brown trout fishing try the Borve Lodge estate.

While on the subject of Scotland's outlying islands all the island systems off Scotland's north coast have tremendous trout fishing and Orkney's lochs of Harray, Stenness, Swannay, Hundland and Boardhouse have a huge reputation for excellent brown trout. I have made a number of visits to the Orkney Isles and have never failed to be delighted by the spirited wild trout residing there. Harray is one of my favourite lochs in Scotland and it holds sea trout and wild browns of tremendous quality and of a good average weight. Though this loch recently had a succession of environmental problems with poor water clarity and an overgrowth of Canadian pond weed, it seems to have recovered and fished well again in 1994. Adjacent Loch Stenness is tidal, brackish water and can be dour but if you catch one it will nearly always be large and exceptionally strong. Note that though these larger lochs see most of the action the small waters can also hold excellent fish and for real excitement catch the small ferry to some of the other outlying islands and cast for big, wild trout in extraordinarily remote places. There is free fishing in all Orkney waters; however, as the local Orkney Association work strenuously and tirelessly to restock waters, paying a small fee toward joining the Association helps cover some of their costs.

The remoter Shetland Isles also appear to burst at the seams with trout lochs, many rarely fished and the quality and size of fish there can be quite outstanding. Shetland has a different feel when compared with the delights of Lewis and Harris. The trout fishing and the scenery is just as outstanding (and just as windswept!) but there is somehow a more affluent air about Shetland, an influence from the nearby oil installations perhaps. Interlinking small islands comprise Shetland and together they have around a thousand trout lochs and sea trout voes (narrow saltwater inlets usually harbouring silver beauties). A thriving local AC, the Shetland Anglers' Association based in Lerwick, has fishings on numerous diverse lochs, the most well-known of which are Spiggie, Clousta, Benston and Tingwall. Further information and an excellent brochure and guidebook can be had direct from the AC secretary and from the Shetland Tourist office.

Back on the mainland again, if we go further north of Ullapool and its Hebridean ferry, we find Wester Ross and the wild districts of Coigach and Glencanisp are favourite haunts of anglers with big lochs like Sionascraig, Fionn, Lurgain, Cam and Veyatie lying in wide glens with spectacular mountain backdrops. The hills are particularly fine here rising up like great volcanoes from a flat rolling moor. It is around the 'airts and pairts' of Elphin that Rosshire meets with that most famed of fishing counties – Sutherland. This well-known angling county is quite simply a sportsman's paradise and with its 2000 or so waters would take several lifetimes to fish properly. It is impossible for me to describe this area fully but the principal attractions include the myriad of lochs in the Lochinver, Kylestrome, Scourie and Durness areas to the western seaboard, and along the northern coast, Tongue, Bettyhill and Melvich also have some superb hill lochs. Inland, the areas of Achfary, Inchnadamph, Lairg, Shin, Strath Oykel, Altnaharra, Kinbrace and Forsinard are renowned brown trout districts and along the eastern quarter there are hill lochs in the Dornoch, Brora, Helmsdale and Golspie areas. Much of this sprawling wild county is underlaid with very fertile limestone deposits and many of the lochs are fed from mineral-rich springs, consequently the growth rates of trout can be quite substantial. Do not always equate towering mountains with a barren infertile land, there are many secret lochs with trout of goodly size hidden within the Sutherland hill ranges!

That about brings me to my home area of Caithness the most northerly county on the British mainland and this truly puts the icing on a magnificent trout fishing cake. It is a county of subtle change after the rugged interiors of Sutherland and it is dotted with fertile 'limestone' lochs, the principal of which include Lochs Watten, Calder, St Johns, Heilan and Scarmclate. Most of Caithness has an underlay of limestone also known locally as 'marl', and consequently the size of the trout is excellent in most of these fertile waters. Equally exciting are some of the smaller, less well-known Caithness lochs, but your friendly tackle shops in the area will advise on this. Put it this way, I could not have picked a better choice for a wild trout area to live in if I had tried!

*   *   *

Selecting a fly beneath the grandeur of Ben Loyal, Sutherland.

Summarising the trout lochs of Scotland like this is of course an almost thankless task for whenever I mention one loch another springs just as readily to mind so though I will return during the course of this book to specific examples of lochs and their districts, let me sum up the pleasures of wild trout angling in Scotland by stating that anything and everything is possible for the trout angler in a country of such diverse waters. You will almost certainly get back from your fishing most of what you desire and much of what you deserve, it is that kind of place. You can choose to pursue wild loch trout at the very lightest level, coming north on the family holiday only once a year or perhaps just fishing locally as a 'fair-weather' angler casting an infrequent line on one or two lochs in your district. This type of fishing is not 'heavyweight' but is still very worthwhile, an hour on a remote hill loch in the company of spirited fish, breathtaking wildlife and scenery is worth a whole day in a frantic office environment. Or then again you may choose to fish on a much more involved level and become an 'expert' on a specific area, a particular water or a particular style of fishing. Fishing for Scotland's brown trout can be as dramatic, as relaxing, as remote or as companionable as you want. I personally like the demands of hunting a wild creature in his own element, facing difficult conditions in solitude and silence and I relish the glorious uncertainties of sometimes succeeding and sometimes not. There is no other sport which can come halfway to producing such challenges, but maybe I am a bit perverse in wanting that, who knows?

Responsible freedom to roam is still at present an inherent right for those who seek the high and lonely places of Scotland*. This independence to do as you (reasonably) please is also part of the enigmatic appeal of trout fishing. All I would ask is that you fish fairly and without avarice, follow local rules and pay for permission as and where appropriate, usually it is a small price to pay for enjoying such an important national angling asset.

I leave you with one example of the extraordinarily powerful appeal of wild trout angling in Scotland. Towards the end of the 1994 season I had occasion to act as a guide for a visiting angler from Australia who wanted to visit some trout lochs close by my home. As we trekked out to these lonely, isolated tarns Richard Wakelin told me of his twenty-year obsession to revisit our remote area, a favourite place of his which he had first come to know as a boy, fishing with his parents and grandparents in the 1960s and 70s. Such were the clarity of his happy memories he could still remember the exact spots where the boats were anchored, what the best flies were and where the trout were likely to be, all as if he had visited the lochs only yesterday. It was with some heady anticipation therefore that we climbed the last cluster of hills and breathlessly reaching the high plateau the waters suddenly lay before us, twinkling lights in a soft sunlit breeze. 'This is a pilgrimage for me,' he said softly but he did not need to say anything, words were superfluous, I could see it in his eyes that somehow he felt he had come home. He carried with him his grandmother's lovely old cane rod together with some equally well-used traditional flies and these he went on to use with the kind of reverence usually reserved only for spiritual occasions. It did not seem to matter that the trout were few that day nor that the weather was unkindly bright, the importance of the day was enough.

It is my firm belief that any passion that can compel a man to come halfway round the world after an absence of twenty years to revisit isolated lochs high on a desolate moor must be something uniquely special. But then again the enigmatic attraction of catching wild trout in wild places will do that to you. Prime yourself with the information in this book and go now and create a few places of pilgrimage for yourself.

* There have been changes in the Criminal Justice Act 1994 which may affect anglers who choose to venture on Scottish land unannounced and without proper permission (see also legal aspects, Chapter 11).

3
A Contrast of Lochs

The first law of ecology is that everything is related to everything else.
BARRY COMMONER

Any visitor cannot help but notice that the number and variety of lochs available for trout fishing in Scotland quickly becomes mind-boggling. This great diversity of waters is exciting and awe-inspiring all at once, even knowing where to begin can be extremely daunting. I can still recall my first youthful visit to the hill lochs of Wester Ross, an area bulging with wonderful trout waters. Overwhelmed by the sumptuous choice I failed to catch much at all, for just as I would plump for one loch my companions would urge another and considerable time-wasting was the inevitable result. Like children let loose in a huge sweetie shop of lochs we rushed headlong from one water to the next hardly pausing for breath; strained calf muscles and a fairly empty fish bass are what I remember most from that excursion. Self-inflicted wounds but happy times nevertheless!

It is this huge contrast of waters which is perhaps the principal attraction of brown trout fishing in Scotland. There are limestone lochs, peaty tarns, marl-based basins, high corrie lochs, glacial troughs, shallow lochs with sandstone shores and waters with such mixed ecology they merit complete books on their own!

Basically, everything which is around, in and under the loch surface will affect the quality of trout within it and this is an essential part of their intrigue. If there is one piece of advice I can safely give you about ascertaining the quality of a loch it is to never assume anything about the water you have chosen for all lochs are not the same even if they lie side by side within a few yards of one another! Indeed one of the most frequent questions I am asked by the visitor confronted by so many Highland waters is, 'How do you know why one loch has good trout in it and why another does not?' I would love to answer that by saying it is all down to my natural brilliance as a trout angler, but actually it has more to do with being able to read and assess the surrounding loch environment than it does with any guru like abilities!

Assessing Loch Environments

A number of critical factors affecting your fishing can actually be determined from the nature of the loch surroundings including the inherent food supply and the likely average size of the fish population. To help you assess the potential of your chosen loch it may assist to think about your eventual goal, the wild trout, as a creature lying at the heart of a much bigger picture (see Fig. 1). Even from this very simple illustration it becomes obvious that the eventual average weight of trout you are likely to catch is directly dependent on what is going on, in and around the fish's immediate environment.

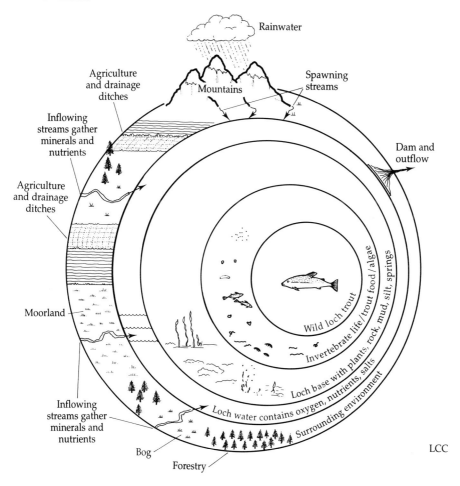

To start with the external influences first, we see the sources of the loch beginning high in the hills as springs and streams gush forth to form the first stages of water catchment. The surrounding environment may be fertile with alkaline-based soil or nutrient-poor, acid peat and as these springs and streams run over the land down to the loch they will gather what nutrients, minerals and salts they can. The rocks may be hard and insoluble, acid like granite, crumbly sandstone or soft dissolving limestone; again these will leach minerals into the water subtly altering its chemistry. If the main watercourse gathers influxes of water from bogs or peatlands the character of the water can be very dark and acidic supporting little invertebrate life. However note that bogs are not all 'bad news' as the various mosses and peat deposits characteristic of marshland fulfil an important role by acting as slowly absorbing giant sponges gathering up the rainwater and giving it a more even dispersal and also assisting in the prevention of sudden destructive spates in the high spawning burns. Rainwater runoff and its associated man-made additives like 'acid rain' will further add to a watery melting-pot of feeder burns and their character may alter several times leaping from nutrient poor to over enriched before they reach the main loch. The inflowing streams gather nutrients and minerals which may help in enriching the final destination but they may also gather unwanted silt or gravel from eroded banks and additionally, green slime algae may be produced if the current is very slack. All these unwanted products have a negating effect on water quality, suffocating most things caught in their path and rendering important trout spawning redds (gravelly runs in feeder streams, used by trout to deposit their spawn) useless.

Once the streams have reached their final destination the *mélange* of dissolved salts, silt and nutrients tips into the main body of the loch. Here everything mixes and mingles providing, for better or for worse, the trout's natural habitat, the water itself. The term 'water quality' is often used to analyse a rather grey area but good 'water quality' for brownies seems to me to mean the loch's capability to provide essential factors governing trout survival. Basically the water must be reasonably pure, reasonably fertile, have a stable cool rather than hot temperature, have good oxygen-holding capabilities and be of a pH which is neither extremely acid nor very alkaline. Though each loch will have differing qualities most of Scotland's waters can sustain reasonably good populations of fish and the number of lochs which are devoid of fish from deoxygenation, pollution or acidification is in the minority rather than the majority.

Regarding the pH of lochs it is important to recognise that in very general terms fish growth is better in 'hard', more alkaline waters than it is in the 'soft', acidic lochs, but I must emphasise this is a widespread rule of thumb and as we have already seen, so many other factors have to be taken into account. Frost and Brown recorded a number of experiments in *The Trout* (1967) on fertilisation of acidic waters carried out by the Scottish Freshwater Fisheries laboratory and other groups, and they also analysed trout growth rates according to pH values. Their scientific research reinforced the theory

Loch water temperature and altitude above sea level can affect trout growth.

that alkalinity is better than acidity but that it is only one influencing factor amongst many and that any fertilisation of waters to increase trout and invertebrate growth had to be sustained over lengthy periods and carefully monitored, otherwise the water quickly reverted to its original acid state.

Water temperature of any loch is critical in that volatile temperature swings from hot to cold can be life-threatening particularly to very young trout and sustained high temperatures can be fatal. Most larger lochs exhibit some water stratification during long summer months when, given reasonably still conditions, a warmer layer of water separates and lies above a deep cold layer rather like oil floating on the water surface. This can have quite a drastic effect on the quality of trout fishing as formerly free-rising trout usually caught by the angler on or near the loch surface suddenly seem to disappear completely. The angler will usually then roundly pronounce the fishing has 'gone off' or is as 'dead as a dodo' when in fact the trout are still there but are lying much deeper than normal to secure cooler habitats.

How the bulk of water in a loch is physically contained is also important. A great many of Scotland's lochs are used as reservoirs and/or are also used to generate electricity in hydroelectric schemes. Whether providing power or water to drink many lochs have had dams placed upon them to form artificially large volumes of water. The flooding of surrounding farmland associated with the original hydro schemes initially brought many new food sources into the lochs and trout growth was quite spectacular in the beginning. However after some years the growth rate reverted to a normal pattern and the long-term benefits of dams did not, on the whole, prove much more beneficial than leaving the water untouched. Today on certain reservoirs, if heavy draw-offs of water are required, significant alteration in the character of the bank vegetation can clearly be seen. Normal trout-feeding areas dry out, vegetation dies and barren stone shores are the norm.

Also note that as a very general guide the altitude the loch is above sea-level will often affect the size of fish present, high lochs tending to produce smaller fish. The poor old trout living in the high corrie lochs often have to fight that much harder to survive colder temperatures though note this is not always the case, other influences such as the fertility of the loch base and the number of spawning streams will also come into play. Additionally you should be aware that the common assumption that the further north a loch is situated the lower its productivity is basically nonsense, and if you come to the limestone lochs of Caithness or north Sutherland I will happily prove the worth of that old chestnut!

The loch base plays the most critical part in determining the eventual fish size. Shallow lochs lying in 'basins' are usually more productive than lochs lying in deep glacial troughs which have a sterile, icy cold core of water supporting little aquatic life. If the bottom of the loch is of a fertile nature such as limestone or marl, even quite acidic runoff from peat drainage or similar can be neutralised and a fish population will normally thrive. Most people think of limestone as chalk as seen in the white cliffs of Dover or the South Downs and by comparison assume the northern Highlands to be barren wastes of bog and peat, yet limestone derivatives are to be found all over Scotland. They vary in texture greatly – anything from organic skeletal remains of organisms like shell sand, to clays, chalky substances and harder rocks which can be polished to make attractive marble. Rocks at Assynt in Sutherland were once extensively quarried for shaping into marble stone-work and lochs in Caithness were once dredged for their lime-bearing mud which was then spread on agricultural fields. Large lime kilns where the lime was extracted from soil to form a powder, are still to be found in the county, though they are now disused.

While any limestone derivative is welcome it is not an absolute essential for the growth of quality wild trout. Lochs with mixed areas of aerated gravel, plants, mud, rocks, sand and silt, with the accent on the former rather than the latter, are also very productive. Although some softer soils are useful as they support a number of burrowing insects including the burrowing mayfly nymph, lochs which have a completely uniform bottom of mud and its associated plants, do not sustain trout populations so well as those with gravel and rock shores. A complete base of silt creates murky deoxygenated water and wild trout do not flourish well in these conditions. Any areas of sand are usually considered infertile in freshwater lochs and indeed without cover few fish are found there, however glacial sands like those found in waters within Caithness and Sutherland have quantities of dissolved shells within them and are quite mineral-rich particularly in calcium. Lochs on the Hebridean islands and Orkney also exhibit this phenomenon and here they are termed 'machair' lochs and are well known for large trout. It is important to remember that apparently sterile sand-banks are not always a deterrent to good overall fish growth. Also adding further to the mineral content of lochs may be unseen natural springs issuing through from the base rock under the water or at its sides, and these supplement the total volume of water, and depending on what type of strata they have come through, may also enrich the loch.

Good mixed plant growth both within the loch and along its shores, is extremely important for healthy trout for it is here they gain most of their food and acquire shelter from any potential threats. Plants also fulfil the vital, life-giving role of consuming carbon dioxide and giving off oxygen during daylight hours (photosynthesis), though note that too much flora and fauna and associated algae can be potentially harmful as, during the hours of darkness, they absorb back the oxygen and give off toxic carbon dioxide. If this nightly process occurs during lengthy warm spells the oxygen content of the water can fall dangerously low resulting in fish mortality, the trout quite literally being suffocated. A considerable amount of the invertebrate life the trout feed on, emanates from the plants, mud and decaying vegetation on the loch base and these insects and mollusca together with minute algae and phytoplankton make up the last stages in a long linkage of events known as food chains, each link of which has a critical influence on the eventual size and quality of those wild trout. Thus the final size of the trout you can catch depends on the quality of its diet and this aquatic life depends for its survival on the quality of its environment and everything depends on the quality of the water and what it draws up from the surrounding landscape: The key to successful trout growth is keeping a balance in all these environmental links and happily trout themselves are very good indicators of what is happening to their surroundings. In fact they are often used by commercial businesses who have to discharge effluents into watercourses to indicate any changes in water quality, so they fulfil an important environmental monitoring role as well as providing a challenge to all those engaged in fishing for them.

Food Chains

One of the best practical illustrations I have heard on how 'food chains' fit together and go on to directly affect your fishing, is the following, originally explained to me by Alan Joyce, an eminent freshwater biologist from Sutherland. In the northern Highlands a very popular artificial fly is the Red Palmer more commonly known as the Soldier Palmer. This is a multi-purpose fly sometimes used as a general representation of a freshwater shrimp. The artificial is tied with a red body and brown palmered hackle and this structure well represents the reddish body of the shrimp and its trailing legs. *Gammarus* (small freshwater shrimp) are very popular with wild trout and fish consuming them as a staple part of their diet are usually of extremely good quality with a deep red/orange flesh. The shrimp obtains his red body colour from feeding on a microscopic creature called *Diaptomas* which has reddish-orange oil droplets contained within its own body. *Diaptomas* in turn has manufactured these droplets from consuming phytoplankton (minute freshwater algae) which contains yellow and green chlorophyll. Thus tying the artificial fly in that way has fitted in extremely well with the shrimp and his food chain. But the story does not end there for *Gammarus* is only found in lochs where the water is of an alkaline nature and he is extremely sensitive to the quantities of dissolved salts present. Thus he is only present in lochs of an alkaline nature, or in lochs fed from springs emanating from potash-rich feldspar which has a capacity for water enrichment. Shrimp are rarely found in peat-acidic waters, they simply cannot survive. So next time you cast a Soldier Palmer at a rising trout remember the tale of how the fish thinks it is a shrimp in that fertile loch and how *Gammarus* gets his colour!

4

Practical Study of Loch Trout

Secret and self contained, and solitary as an oyster.

CHARLES DICKENS

Strains of Wild Trout

Scientists, predominantly in the Victorian era, classified wild brown trout with lengthy Latin names, complex classes and sub categories. It was then an age of great discovery after all and wild trout strains, real or imagined, were much more to the fore than today when we usually class sea trout and brown trout as *Salmo trutta* and have done with it. Though we have seen that original stocks of Scottish trout have been somewhat adulterated either with new generations of hatchery-reared browns or with the introduction of American fish like the rainbow trout, happily there are a few fisheries where the genetic integrity of the trout is virtually untouched and dotted around Scotland are a number of fish populations unique to their area. These are strains of trout which have grown in relatively isolated habitats for centuries without the interference of man in any way. The shape and beautiful markings of certain genetic strains obviously make them distinctive and easily recognisable even in the 1990s. Specific fish to look out for, apart from the huge number of varieties of *Salmo fario* (common brown trout), include *Salmo Levenensis* (Loch Leven strain), *Salmo ferox* (great lake trout) and in the Highlands some more unusual classes like the yellow trout, the parr-marked trout or the hump-backed trout.

In most areas of the country, the strain of trout most frequently sought and caught by anglers is *Salmo fario*, more simply termed *Salmo trutta* today. In the past this fish has had a string of other localised names including the 'burn' or 'river' trout and is known in Gaelic as *breac*, indeed there are a considerable number of lochs in the far north called *Loch nam Breac* (see Appendix 2). The common *fario* strain of trout is the most widespread and is characterised by its black and red speckled markings dotted along golden iridescent flanks with a pale underbelly and darker back. These markings can be remarkably mixed however for some trout are heavily speckled with spots, some have large circular black rings, some with lots of red spots, some with hardly any, but all are extremely beautiful. Most trout show a

Well hooked, a beautifully marked mature wild brown of 3lb 2oz.

remarkable ability to blend their body colour to match their natural surroundings and they have chameleon-like qualities apparently able to disappear into nothing, not least when you are fishing for them! Trout in dark-bottomed lochs can be almost black, whereas trout in light, clear water perhaps with a pale sandstone or limestone bottom, tend to be silver or gold in colour with green or very light brown dorsal regions.

The Loch Leven trout is an exquisitely marked fish, silver flanked and speckled with black asterisk spots. It has been successfully stocked into various waters worldwide including as far away as New Zealand. Leven trout have become quite commonplace around many parts of Scotland and in the past Scottish hatchery owners frequently imported Leven fish into their own brood stock. The wild trout hatchery at Ardgay, Sutherland, apparently successfully reared Leven fish until around the 1950s and these trout were then used to restock a number of remote northern lochs. It is interesting to note however, that there are also naturally occurring populations of almost identically marked fish, closely resembling the silver beauties of Fife but not thought to be descendants of imported fish. For example the silvery trout from Loch Borralie and Loch Croispol at Durness also have 'Leven' markings as do the trout of Loch Watten in Caithness, Loch Harray on Orkney and Loch Spiggie in Shetland. In the 1800s Loch Croispol even had a strain of trout named after it, the 'Crasaphuil' trout. Even allowing for man's past restocking efforts quite why this particular silvery strain of fish is so scattered around Scotland is intriguing and the answer seems to lie in the nature of the loch environment. All the aforementioned waters are quite similar in ecology being very fertile with a pale base rock with clear alkaline water and all have profuse sub-surface feeding with high concentrations of shrimp. If indeed brown trout are the non-migratory descendants of sea trout which became landlocked, the Loch Leven strain closely resembles its migratory sea-going brethren. In fact at freshwater Loch Borralie, Durness, which on first viewing from the hills looks all the world like an aquamarine blue sea loch, I would argue that it is almost impossible to tell whether its shining fish are sea trout or browns.

The *Salmo ferox* (lake trout) is a large deepwater trout who feeds almost exclusively on shoals of Arctic charr together with any smaller brown trout coming his way. They are fierce predatory beasts with cannibalistic tendencies growing to hefty sizes, anything from around 5–20lb (2–9 kg) in weight, and are a significantly longer-living fish than ordinary brown trout. They tend to inhabit deep glacial lochs which are not overly rich in nutrients and minerals, and seem to have adapted their lifestyle to cope with a normally harsh and difficult trout environment. Recent research suggests that ferox travel some distance, perhaps following shoals of charr, and do not tend to linger in a small territory like their brown trout brethren.

It is said that ferox are rarely caught by methods other than trolling, but this is not strictly true for I have caught only one ferox in my angling career on a very large, fluffy dry fly. Unfortunately I lost it as I tried to beach it over a boulder-strewn shore and cried for a week! (See also Chapter 7.) Most of the bigger lochs of Scotland have ferox present and they include Fionn Loch, Lochs Awe, Calder, Assynt, Arkaig, Lomond, Rannoch, Ness, Ericht, Garry and Monar amongst others. A number of these unusual big trout end up looking more like pike with large serrated teeth and snake-like body, but not all grow like that and some remain stunningly well marked and beautifully shaped with deep golden flanks. In Frost and Brown's book, *The Trout*, they are of the belief that ferox are merely trout which have grown to extra-large proportions, but quite why some are ugly, almost kelt-like, and others remain well marked is not fully understood. Unattractive or beautiful, they are a force to be reckoned with in any angler's book – a tussle with a ferox can last a good hour and the tackle must be able to take the strain.

Other trout populations still more or less genetically intact include a population of 'yellow trout' which are known to still exist in a remote loch chain in Sutherland. These trout, with very few spots resemble bars of gold with a golden back and are rarely found outwith that area, though just occasionally something similar is caught from a loch in Caithness, a most unusual and beautiful fish. Equally intriguing is the class of fish known as *Salmo cornubiensis* or 'parr-marked' trout. In 1887 the great natural historian

Harvie Brown made reference to this distinctive fish emanating from a lochan in the Reay Forest of Sutherland and remarked that they had unusual grey finger-mark patches on their flanks which disappeared after death. I have encountered a similarly marked fish in the 1990s in a loch in central Caithness, so it would seem safe to say that the strain still exists and that it comes from some of the oldest known stocks of trout in the northern Highlands. Harvie Brown also refers to the 'hump-backed' trout of central Sutherland, an example he states, of the isolation of the fish population causing a genetic deformity. I have no reason to doubt that they may still exist because of their extreme remoteness, though I am unsure whether another strain listed as 'gillaroo', also known as *Salmo stomachicus*, can still be found in Scotland today. Originally the gillaroo came from Ireland but a population existed for a time in Loch Mulach Corrie near Assynt in Sutherland. They were a particularly beautiful fish with a coloration similar to deepwater charr with reddish-crimson flanks and green backs and had an extra thick stomach wall to cope with a diet of snail and other crustaceans. As the staple diet of a number of fish populations in the Highlands and elsewhere is predominantly snail and shrimp, quite why other brown trout do not develop thick stomach walls remains a mystery.

Basic Anatomy

While the exterior markings of loch trout are delightfully mixed, the anatomy of the wild trout does not vary much. Basically our loch trout are beautifully proportioned with dynamic torpedo-shaped bodies designed to withstand turbulent water and they are built primarily for speed and agility. They are highly adaptable to most types of environment and can exist in all but very warm and/or heavily polluted waters. They usually only grow to a size which can be sustained by the amount of food available in their territory. If food is in short supply, for example in an exposed, windswept mineral-deficient loch with little mixed vegetation, the trout population present there is likely to average a constant half a pound or less. But if you remove some of these small trout and place them in a water with a more abundant food supply, where there is less stress placed upon them and less competition for food, their average size can increase quite significantly.

In most lochs, even if the apparent average weight is on the small side, perhaps less than half a pound, you will usually find there are a few bigger specimens present. Their larger size may usually be put down to their adapting their feeding behaviour to encompass a particularly rich food source either not commonly eaten by the rest of the fish population or not present elsewhere in the loch. This could be the finding of a fertile inflowing

A torpedo-shaped body designed for speed and agility.

spring often full of fat caddis cases which the fish then guards jealousy as 'his' territory, or the fish may have latched on to feeding on his own kind in cannibalistic fashion perhaps eating tiny trout fry, sticklebacks or a coarse fish such as perch. Such fish are not necessarily ferox for they may be found in shallow lochs without charr, they are just hefty trout who have led a lifestyle of good food and unstressful living!

Fish Behaviour

Scotland's wild brown trout are normally solitary, non-shoaling fish lying within their own quite precise territories for most of the season. In lochs, territories can range from a square yard to perhaps six square yards, and it should be noted that each water will offer slightly different sizes of fish territory. For example where there is an over abundance of small fish their individual domain can be correspondingly small but in a loch with fewer, larger fish they will range over a wider area but always as individuals rather than in a shoal. Because many of our visitors have become accustomed to the habits of rainbow trout which normally cruise around a stillwater in close-knit groups, they assume our wild trout will do the same. Of course they do not, for they much prefer their own lies rather like the salmon, and they opt if possible for their 'lie' to be adjacent to both an abundant larder and a safe bolt-hole. Though in all cases the brown trout favours isolation there are certain lochs which have populations of what are commonly known as 'free-rising' fish, that is trout which show themselves on the surface frequently, while other lochs gain reputations for dour, silent waters where hardly anything breaks the surface and it is quite possible for the angler to assume there are no fish present there at all. This type of behaviour where trout appear to favour one depth of water over another is largely dictated by the whereabouts of the trout's main sources of food. If the biggest food supply happens to be on the water surface the trout are there, if it happens to be near the bottom that is where they linger, it is as simple as that.

Very few wild trout exhibit any shoaling 'safety in numbers' behaviour, but there are particular times of year when brown trout can give the appearance of shoal movements. I have seen some really fantastic cruising of large trout taking place during the prolific mayfly hatch in Caithness when what appears to be shoals of brownies move in unison toward the shore often in water less than two feet deep, gobbling up mayfly as they emerge in nymph form or alight on the water after a first stuttering flight. Equally, I have also observed big brown trout apparently hunting in packs after the shoals of tiny stickleback fry when the new-born of this small fish are profuse in the loch in late July. It is easy for someone briefly seeing this type of behaviour to assume it happens all year round when it is actually governed by the appropriate seasonal time. Unfortunately for much of the year the wild trout is safely out of sight, in areas of good feeding and adequate shelter. In very general terms our wild trout will usually favour the shallower margins at anything from 2–10ft (60 cm–3m) is the norm for wild trout and the angler should first seek him there, often the complete opposite to reservoir rainbow fishing tactics where I have often seen fishers determinedly keel hauling sunk lines off dam walls out into the very deepest part of the water.

Because of the generally harsher environment of the northern hemisphere the brown trout try determinedly to expend as little energy as possible, either in chasing food or in gaining shelter from any perceived threat. Energy conservation is both vital for survival and to enable the fish to achieve any decent increase in size and body weight. Thus trout in exposed high-altitude lochs without a prolific food source will tend to remain lean and small throughout their lifetime as they have to work much harder to attain a normal weight.

Though the trout can sometimes be short of food they are rarely short of that other vital resource, oxygen. Most of our lochs receive a fair battering of gales and wind and vigorous wave action is generally sufficient to well oxygenate small and large waters alike. Like their river cousins swimming upstream, loch trout usually face into the wind for maximum oxygen over their gills and also to enable them to be first to any tasty morsel blown offshore. Loch trout are non-migratory except when they leave their usual lies to migrate *en masse* for the purposes of spawning away from the main loch on 'redds' in the feeder burns, a process which usually starts toward the end of October.

Natural Spawning

Spawning is the one time of year when wild trout throw all caution to the wind leaving their usual territories to collect *en masse* at the nearest burn mouth ready to spawn. This fantastic migration is in fact rarely seen by the angler as it occurs outwith the trout season, normally during the period mid-October to mid-November. In 1994, at the season's end, I spent many days at our loch recording the fascinating movements of the wild fish, a quite awe-inspiring sight worth relating as it is so rarely observed in the natural state.

By 21 October, I found a great number of trout were cruising around the mouth of the inflowing burn and then suddenly, two days later, after a day of torrential rain they rushed in great waves up the inflowing burn and on up into the remotest ditches, springs and rivulets they could find. To stand and watch seemingly endless bow waves of fish weave and splash their

Natural spawning. With backs out of the water the wild trout rush up the tiny spawning burn.

way up to the very source of the burn was one of the most thrilling moments of my angling career, all without lifting a rod or casting a fly. I watched intently as most trout, many with backs and dorsal fins clearly out of the water, headed straight to the purest flow of an underground spring where they gathered in water not more than a foot deep. I watched a female flipping on her side casting up the gravel to dig out her nest for the eggs, the male all the time at her flank nudging and encouraging her, then, in quick darting movements the pair would slide forward together to procreate over the excavated redds. To one side another single male lay in wait trying as best he could to sidle in on the act but no, the protective male would have none of it and slashed viciously at any of his intrusions. Once the eggs and milt were safely deposited the female covered the redd with the gravel, burying the newly fertilised eggs quite deeply with some surprisingly hefty chunks of gravel. Little wonder the tails and fins of fish which have recently spawned have a ragged appearance, heaving those lumps of gravel around is demanding work! Whilst so engaged in the business of reproduction the trout completely ignored my close proximity and it was an uplifting and wonderful sight to see the species literally continuing itself beneath my feet, something I shall never forget.

October and November are generally the most favoured months for wild trout spawning, I recorded with assistance from other local enthusiasts trout present on the redds between 23 October and 1 November; other observations were made later in the month of November but no further trout were seen on the main redds in 1994. The exact stimulus which made them migrate *en masse* up the burn is not easy to pinpoint however; it seems to have been a rise in water height coupled with a corresponding increase in flow following heavy rain. The evenings before trout were observed in full daylight on redds had been frosty and moonlit, thus it is also possible that another trigger which guides trout to spawn is a drop in air temperature. It is important to note however, that not all trout follow the text books and that large trout have been found on redds ready to spawn in the middle of June, equally I have caught a number of female trout in May full of several years' eggs in our own loch where the natural spawning was observed. These fish had been completely unable to spawn or to reabsorb their eggs for some time and as sea trout they would be called baggots, a very odd occurrence and the subject of much speculation by the natural historians amongst us. Eventually after considerable deliberations we decided that once the older, mature trout reached a size of around 1lb 12oz (800g) they became physically too big to reach the very small area of spawning redds available. Thus a goodly majority of the larger fish failed to shed eggs as there simply was not enough room for them on redds only 10in (25 cm) across in some places. All the fish seen on the redds in October 1994 were not more than about 1lb (450g) or so in weight and many were around 3/4lb

(340g); during our period of observation we saw no fish larger than 1lb 8oz (675g). Another less likely theory for these baggot fish, was that there were not enough males in the population to stimulate the females into egg laying, but this was not as likely a hypothesis as a good many smaller males were found accompanying like-sized females in the October spawning and could in fact accompany the larger females if required. A simple management measure decided upon for next summer will be to physically widen and deepen the top spawning area and add further gravel chunks to its base as it was felt that if the redds were enlarged this may encourage the larger hen fish of over 1lb 8oz to come up to spawn.

In general you will know if trout are ready to spawn from their condition. The females have bulbous flabby stomachs heavy with eggs and the males have darkened in colour, often with kyped jaws and extruding milt when you lift them. Anal fins can be tipped with a bright white edging which is said to show fish in readiness to spawn though note I have found fish with whitened fins in lochs in mid-July and I put it down to general wear and tear on the lower fins as the trout held its station very close to the bottom. Also present on spawning fish is an extra coating of mucus which makes the trout very slimy and difficult to pick up. This extra mucus appears on the fish as early as the beginning of September and acts as insulation and protection from the coming winter chills. I have the theory that if the impending winter is going to be very cold then the trout seem to anticipate this, producing thicker, slightly opaque mucus than if the winter is likely to be mild. This idea has been borne out from the last five years of records, however there is always a maverick to confound even the most sound of theories! Equally it is possible to tell when air and water temperatures have consistently risen, usually during May, for this extra winter coat dissipates and the trout return to a normal shining condition.

Wild trout prefer the cleanest, fastest flow of water to spawn in and prefer even gravel sites with the size of stones not much bigger than small plums. Sites with too much sand or mud are of little use as the eggs are quickly suffocated; equally flat, hard slabs of rock are not chosen as no redds can be excavated in such a surface. Upper streams with a fairly consistent water height are selected first over streams or ditches which dry out quickly without rain. If there are no suitable sites to spawn either in inflowing or outflowing burns then the wild trout may excavate redds in gravel beds within the loch itself nearly always on a well-oxygenated side of the water. For example if the prevailing wind is south-west then the redds may be found on the north-east shore where wave action constantly oxygenates the eggs. Not all mature trout choose to spawn every year, indeed some may only spawn every second year and these trout make good over-wintered fish and may be caught by the angler near normal food and shelter sources.

Jimmy Gunn and Andrew Crawford dig out the flat stones from the burn to assist winter spawning.

The length of time eggs take to mature and become small *fry* varies from water to water and is largely governed by temperature. A rise in temperature accelerates growth in the embryo, a drop slows it down. In the most general of terms if the eggs are on the nest in late October and the water temperature stays fairly constant at 6°C then the incubation time for eggs to become alevins is likely to be about eleven or twelve weeks later depending on the severity of the winter. Frost and Brown in *The Trout* indicated that feeding fry can be seen in the burns or near their spawning sites as early as March if there has been a mild winter. Unfortunately these tiny fry are very vulnerable and few survive; as a rough guide for every 800 eggs fertilised only twenty of those will survive to become one-year-old trout. Depending on rainfall the fry may spend a considerable time in the spawning stream or may be forced back into the main loch. Certainly in my own loch I have observed an apparent rush of fry to main loch feeding grounds in June with the burn in low water conditions, and I presume from the parr markings of these tiny fish that they are the new batch of maturing fry.

Given such harsh winter conditions in which to reproduce it is a wonder the wild trout survives at all but survive he does and in quite some number in specific areas around Scotland. It is my belief that natural spawning should always be encouraged and assisted where possible, for nature can usually do its work given a proper chance. Only if the wild rearing process irretrievably breaks down should those with angling interests intervene by restocking of some sort. If a hatchery is considered *in situ* I would hope that the indigenous wild trout strains would be preserved by stripping and using brood stock only from the loch concerned, but those entering into such work should be realistic as any rearing of wild fish is a labour-intensive and time-consuming business. Without the presence of a local hatchery buying in small fingerling trout commercially reared from outside sources is the easiest option, but the end result of such actions is always a dilution of original strains until they are no longer recognisable. However I notice recently that some commercial wild trout farms are willing to take and breed from your own brood stock brought in from your specific area. This is an interesting new development and one those with the wild trout interests at heart may wish to consider in future management measures.

The Diet of Wild Loch Trout

It is important to remember that despite most of our lochs lying in the cooler reaches of the northern hemisphere, many will still produce a profusion of insect and aquatic life of considerable complexity given the correct environmental conditions. 'Hatches' may sometimes occur a little later in the year but happen they do and the visiting angler need only allow for some seasonal variations in their timing. Insects like, for example, the prized mayfly actually begin to appear mid-June in the Highlands, much later than their southern chalkstream counterparts. More than once I have scanned entomology books for a particular insect I have encountered locally on lochs in Scotland, only to find it described as being 'local' only to the far south! I mention this not to detract from the respected knowledge already compiled but rather to add the point that the northern environment should neither be neglected nor dismissed outright as barren wastes. In many areas it can be just as productively fertile as that of the south.

It is often assumed that because of the cooler conditions of Scotland, our browns will feed voraciously on anything that moves. This is to a certain extent true for the wild loch trout is indeed an opportunistic feeder, taking at least a good look and possibly a bite at most things which come its way. However, he tempers greed with considerable caution and therefore any reckless food consumption is almost always well kept in check by a compulsive need for security. However, given the right conditions and the urge to feed, he will consume a huge selection of aquatic life; anything from the complete range of nymphal forms to all sorts of beetles, snails and

A Caithness mayfly – mayfly commonly hatch in various areas of the Northern Highlands usually from mid June onward.

shrimps along with copious numbers of winged insects including most varieties of flies from the generic range of midges, stoneflies, sedges, mayflies, olives, caenis, bibios, moths, hawthorn fly, alders and caddis fly. (Note in the generic term 'midge' that we have the usual very wide selection of non-biting 'buzzers' and their pupae but, unfortunately, we also have an unholy abundance of small biting midges hatching from peaty soils in the more dull, humid conditions of July and August. From an angling point of view the former midge is easy to deal with while the latter can make strong men weep in anguish so be warned!)

The loch trout will feed at most depths according to what is seasonally available and he obtains a good proportion of his nourishment from feeding off or near the bottom. This does not necessarily mean the fish are extremely deep-lying, just that they seek the invertebrate life off the shoreline margins, noses down as well as noses up. Practical examination of both the physical size and the quantity of trout fodder available, will give you an indication of the loch fertility and the likely fish size. For example, lochs with profuse numbers of large fat caddis cases or numerous wriggling shrimps almost always contain good trout, whereas lochs with scarce, thin little stonefly nymph populations may be somewhat barren and less productive. From personal observation I have found that lochs with a surfeit of the little beetle *Corixa* almost always have good quality large trout present, however, getting these trout out nearly always turns out to be extremely challenging as the fishing tends to be very dour, perhaps with only one, albeit large, trout achieved in the course of a week's angling.

Look out for the presence of small fish fry in the shallows as some larger trout, particularly those over the pound or so, will become fixated on feeding voraciously on these smaller fish and their young. Sticklebacks and their fry make welcome additional sources of protein as do small coarse fish like perch. It is also possible for big trout to feed on the fry of their own kind, cannibalistic in fact, though they may or may not become 'ferox' because of this tendency. Thus lochs holding prominent numbers of small fry may well hold some very large trout who have grown sleek and fat on their swimming brethren.

Trout have also been known to take small freshwater eels who live in great quantity on the loch floor and feed directly off the bottom. The eels make their appearance in the lochs around April and May when they return from their ocean-going spawning to their feeding grounds in most Scottish freshwaters. Larger trout are said to find them quite a delicacy particularly on Orkney where, I have been told by resident guru Ed Headley, that trout are occasionally caught with eels in their gut.

Apart from consuming food from within the loch itself, either on or near the bottom or when it is rising up nymph-fashion toward the surface, trout will take all manner of airborne insects blown in from the surrounding landscape. These include any of the hatched insects I have already mentioned like the midge, sedge, stonefly or olive, along with others like bumble-bees, bluebottles, damsel-flies, dragonflies, daddy-long-legs and the innocuous cow-dung fly. The latter is a flat-winged brownish insect emanating from very unsavoury sources but it is particularly good for inspiring frantic slashing rises in trout when it is blown onto the water surface. Indeed it is an insect I would place on a high par with the mayfly and the 'daddy' for its extraordinary ability to make trout appear as if they are actively and acrobatically 'shoaling' offshore.

More novel trout tastes include a penchant for small frogs. I once spent a heady morning on a fertile hill loch cleverly matching, or so I thought, the hatch of emerging sedge and I returned home feeling ever so slightly smug at capturing four trout all of around a pound plus. Having loudly proclaimed my skills to the few still listening in a family well used to their mother's exploits, you may imagine my surprise when I gutted the trout to reveal tightly packed frog bones within the stomach of each fish! Apart from graphically illustrating the catholic tastes of brown trout the experience left me soundly chastened. I quietly vowed not to crow so loudly of my ability to catch wild trout, for, just when I think I am really getting the hang of it, the fish will again surprise and frequently embarrass me, still that is why I go fishing for them.

The Abundance Factor

The key word to bear in mind when looking at the diet of trout with a view to fishing for them is *abundance*. Where there is likely to be an abundance of invertebrate life there are likely to be plenty of trout close by, but do remember prolific amounts of a specific food item may happen only during certain periods in the year. For example, once the northern mayfly begin to hatch in June trout you did not know were there will surface feed avidly, gobbling up this luscious insect. Once the hatch subsides by mid-August these apparently free-rising fish may well disappear completely from their mayfly hunting grounds and revert back to bottom grubbing. Or, if you look at my embarrassment with the frog-consuming fish, this incident actually occurred at the height of the mating season for wild frogs (normally late April, early May) and the resident brownies had obviously become aware of a prolific food source whirling and splashing in a confined area of the loch. Once the frog mating season subsided far fewer trout where taken by my rod from that bay and no trout were taken with frogs in their stomach contents for the rest of the season.

The appearance of an abundant food supply is vital in stirring trout into action, for instance when the stickleback rearing season is at its height. In the far north, sticklebacks have usually produced their offspring by early August and with the appearance of these profuse shoals in the shallows, brownies may well alter their feeding behaviour to vigorously chase and consume some of the huge numbers of this tiny fish. Such seasonal food appearances I call feeding *triggers*, for while the 'hatch' is occurring the trout are stimulated into greedy almost reckless feeding, often seizing your own artificial with abandon as they plough into struggling mayfly or terrified fry. However once the trigger subsides they revert to more cautious and secretive behaviour. Of course there will be times when insect hatches are so prolific the fish fail to respond to any imitations as for example on Loch Watten, Caithness, where I have found the Caenis hatches of late June to be so overpowering, the fish generally refuse to look at any artificial no matter how cleverly devised; but generally speaking the best fishing times will correspond with when the fish are *actively feeding*.

For consistent angling success therefore, I would normally advise making some attempt to find the most *abundant* food source likely to *trigger* fish into action for once the usually cautious wild trout become obsessed with consuming that month's particular menu they do relax their inbred canniness slightly, and placing your artificial amongst the action will usually bring results.

Safe Houses

If it were possible to view a clearwater loch from above, looking straight down through it to the trout's habitat, you would almost always find the fish lying next to a convenient bolt-hole. Underwater features like weed beds, big boulders, overhanging banks, drop-off ledges, old tree stumps,

Fishing the sheltered shallows. Wild trout in the wildest of places.

broken walls or fences, provide the ideal safe environment for wild trout. At the slightest hint of anything unusual occurring in the fish's world such as a flash of light, a hefty vibration or a sudden movement that does not correspond to the normal run of things, the trout will head straight for this cover. The chosen underwater safety features also provide them with a good source of food for such rocks and weeds create a safe harbour for all sorts of invertebrate life. Security is vital in a world where predators include pike, diving birds like cormorant or northern diver, otter and heron and where the most skilled predator is nearly always man.

Not always considered by visiting anglers who cannot see the effect of a year's weather on a loch, is the fact that much of a trout's life is spent seeking shelter from the onslaught of winter and thus bolt-holes may vary in position according to the elements. After a long, hard off-season you may well encounter trout lingering in the most sheltered, fertile areas of the loch. They will have taken up position behind rocks or weeds sometimes in only a foot or so of water and thus in March and April incautious wading is not desirable, you quite simply scare away everything in sight! On a number of occasions with the season just under way, I have found trout lingering virtually under my feet and have noted this side-clinging behaviour continuing until the beginning of June if the spring is very cold. As the rainfall decreases and temperatures increase through the angling year, the trout's shallow bolt-holes will quite literally dry out and they have to move offshore to re-establish their territories beside new and safer underwater features. I call this phenomenon the 'flitting' (a Scots word for moving house!) and though it will happen at slightly different times of the year according to rainfall it will almost always have occurred by the end of June.

Maintaining energy reserves also becomes vital for survival during very bad winters when food may be in short supply, and particularly after the rigours of spawning, the trout will always seek comfort and shelter to recuperate, away from the more exposed and gale-battered areas of the loch.

5

Fishing on the Trout Lochs

Don't ever take a fence down until you know why it was put up.

ROBERT FROST

As we know, Scotland's wild loch trout have a huge and important place in our angling history with the great traditions of 'loch-style' angling going back to such illustrious pioneers as 'Black Palmer' of the 1800s with his greenheart rods and silken lines. Today loch-style tackle and techniques are used on waters all over the British Isles and though the fishing gear has raced into the twentieth century with many advances made in tackle design and high-technology materials, the tactical style of loch fishing has not dramatically changed. I for one am rather glad of this for I like my fishing to have a sense of ethic and history, and want any twentieth-century improvements to assist my angling ability without detracting from its original Scottish identity. I am not such a traditionalist that I will ignore modern fibres which keep me warmer, new materials for rods or lines which make me cast more accurately or better waders to keep me drier, but I do like the feeling of following in the path of an important Scottish angling heritage laid down by many more worthy than myself. Good loch trout fishing is a combination of simple yet beautifully skilful, established techniques and when I am tutoring loch fishing I try never to overcomplicate what is a pure and honest craft. To do so is to introduce a pomposity into the sport which should never exist. To let you also enjoy the challenges and the lovely simplicity of our sport you have to start somewhere and let us take a look at a selection of basic equipment to set you off.

Loch-style Tackle

Recently I have noticed more and more British rod manufacturers calling their rods 'loch style', so much so that I often have complete beginners arriving on my Highland doorstep with expensive powerful 12ft (3.7m) rods but with little or no idea how to use them. It is quite true that in days past very long rods of up to 16ft (5m) or more were used to catch brown trout, however these slowly fell from favour to a length of around 10ft (3m) during my angling lifetime. It is only comparatively recently that competition anglers have revived the longer rods as a way to better catches, stating that they feel more in control of both the fish and the aerialising of all that line they throw out with metronomic accuracy. I also suspect they use the longer rods to be able to work the heavy sinking lines frequently used when pursuing rainbow trout, which goes rather against the grain of loch-style floating line fishing!

Youngster hard at work with a through action rod.

I personally use a rod of 10ft (3m) which I consider more than adequate to the task of loch fishing for both brown trout and sea trout and I also use it for low-water salmon but that is another story. If you are a complete beginner to loch-trout fishing I would recommend a rod of around 9–10ft (2.7–3m) made of light carbon fibre or a similar light material. Today carbon fibre rods have dropped in price, though beware of cheap CFs which seem dreadfully floppy and consequently give poor line control. A number of loch devotees still use the old-fashioned split-cane rods and some of these rods are a positive delight to use particularly those known as 'ladies' rods, but note that if you are buying old second-hand cane rods tread warily and try them out with a fly line and reel first, never buy them blind, you could be in for a nasty shock. Not all cane is light and pleasant to use but if you are lucky and find one of sweet action hang on to it for the old traditional materials can still give excellent service.

Regarding the build of the rod I prefer a tip to middle action, fairly stiff but with enough 'give' in it to safely absorb shocks yet propel the line easily across a strong wind. I used to use cheaper through/butt action rods but in the end found I expended too much effort and lost too many fish with a rod which wobbled and waggled alarmingly especially after a year or so's hard use. My choice when selecting a rod is always to ensure it is as light and as sweet-actioned as possible; I become not a little bad-tempered trying to fish with overly heavy rods or with ones that are without spring and unresponsive, still perhaps I am showing my age! In fact I would suggest choosing your rod as you would your fishing partner; I prefer one which is light but not frivolous, lively but kind and preferably never ever dull!

Most modern reels are pleasantly light and well made and when choosing one note that it should 'balance' the rod. Simply explained that means you can pick up the rod with its reel attached easily as one unit without the reel feeling like a dead weight at one end! Basically you will get what you pay for in reels and I would recommend plumping for one which is made of a light metal, capable of withstanding hard use and is easily cleaned and oiled inside. The majority of reels today are like car engines, maintain them well with plenty of lubrication and they will usually serve you for many years.

On to the reel must go the fly line and what a dazzling array of these things there are today compared with those of yesteryear. They come in all weights and sizes and having selected one to match the rod weight, for example my rod requires a 7/8 line, I would advise you start loch fishing for wild trout with a floating line. This is the traditional way and it is undoubtedly also the easiest line to lift off the water surface rather than having to drag it up from the depths. In my own tackle bag there is a spare intermediate line which sinks slightly below the surface and is useful for flat calms and I also have a (rarely used) sinking line, which I have only ever

Top: Beautifully shaped wild trout from a Scottish loch; note the differences in colour and markings, typical of the species which all came from the same small water.

Bottom: The old trout hatchery at Ardgay, Sutherland, once run by the McNicol brothers, was an extensive system of tanks and pens running down to the sea and supplied wild trout to lochs throughout the far North up until the 1960s.

Top: Loch Harray, Orkney and Ed Headley reflects on the end of a successful angling day.

Bottom: World-famous Loch Lomond in tranquil mood.

Loch Calder, Caithness, and a last cast into the setting sun.

Loch Coruisk, Skye, on a stunning day with a mountaineer's paradise of big hills beyond.

Top: Loch Caladail, Sutherland, a gin-clear limestone loch where big trout lurk and anglers are driven mad trying to tempt them!

Bottom: A small trout loch set high in the hills above Tomich, Inverness-shire.

Top: Early morning mist lifts from Loch Voil, Perthshire.

Bottom: Wild trout excavating their redds for natural spawning in October 1994 at the Reay Lochs, Caithness.

Traditional loch-style fishing is normally executed from the boat, but good results are also had from the bank. Loch Watten, Caithness.

Fly-tying is an integral part of our fishing skills and the thrill of catching a trout to a hand-tied pattern should not be under estimated.

Above: Fishing by moonlight! The effects of the weather will often dictate success or failure on the loch.

Right: It is important to develop your tactics according to local requirements. Tactics from around Scotland show broadly similar requirements but each area has one or two subtle variations in technique.

Top: The wild brown trout plays a central role in Scotland's angling heritage and it is vital that it is conserved and properly managed for the benefit of future generations of anglers.

Bottom: Classic Scottish loch fishing – Lesley Crawford casts into the dusking light on a remote Highland loch.

had to ply on lowland Scottish lochs. My fly lines are all weight forward (WF) which means I have a slight advantage if I have to propel them across a strong side wind and since in the Highlands I nearly always have to fish in a gale, WF lines are a secure investment! The spare intermediate and sinking lines are both double taper as their extra weight seems to carry them out on the loch without too much difficulty. Compared with double-tapered lines, it is often claimed weight-forward floaters do occasionally lose something in the presentation of the fly. You might notice this if the wind suddenly drops and your line starts to roll over with a comparatively heavy splash, or does that only happen to me? It is also sometimes said that complete novices will find a WF less easy to handle than a double taper, well yes they do occasionally but not always, and any assistance is better than nothing at all if they are trying to fish across a strong wind. All in all I believe I would never be without a WF line for my often tough Highland conditions and for complete beginners I have either a WF or a DT for them to try for much depends on how they ply the rod and what the wind speed is on the day in question.

The main criterion for the material used to construct my fly line is that it should be supple and pliable, not retain an annoying 'memory' and not crack with wear. Most modern mid-price range fly lines attain these yardsticks reasonably well though I still suffer the odd disappointment, perhaps my 'wear and tear' is much harder than the average user's. To attach the fly line to the reel you will often see an amount of backing recommended. This is a thin nylon cord-like material which allows for an extra section of line if the fish manages to take all your fly line out from the reel on one of his runs. In all honesty I admit I have never been in the situation where the fish has 'stripped line down to the backing' though I have come close to it with wild trout of 5lb (2 kg) or so, but then again I always give the fish only enough line as he needs, preferring to play trout hard and quickly to the net. I have found that giving it some controlled 'welly' is a good enough maxim to follow when playing out fish, kinder to both the trout and to the angler's heart rate!

At the end of the fly line we must attach some nylon and finally the fly and in days past the gut or nylon was simply joined directly to the fly line by a loop or a needle knot. When I teach young children impatiently waiting to cast a first fly I still prefer to use a little knot at the end of the fly line and slip a loop of nylon directly over it to join everything together. I realise such elementary knot tying is not de rigueur in the days of braided leaders, special plastic tubes and other fancy joiners, but you try taking a class of children with frozen fingers and short attention spans in a force nine gale! The use of a braided leader, that is a woven piece of hollow; soft nylon material about 4–5ft long, extends the fly line to a narrow, flexible point on to which the tippet and fly is then attached. To be honest they have brought me mixed

Group discussion of equipment required for a windswept day on Loch Calder, Caithness.

results. I find them useful and they do assist in the roll over of the line, but I do not swear by them, unlike other anglers who would never be without them. Nowadays they are also designed to fast or slow sink below the water surface assisting in a quicker presentation of the fly at the correct depth; they do indeed do all this in calmer conditions but in any wind I cannot say I notice much difference. However, if you think you gain some advantage from them, feel free to use them! Personally if I want more depth or a more secretive presentation of the artificial fly away from the main body of the fly line I tend just to make the nylon longer perhaps by using a piece of thicker 8lb (3.6 kg) nylon tapered down to a loop on to which goes my 4lb (1.8 kg) nylon. This joining mechanism uses the same principal as the other loops and braided leaders but is a lot cheaper.

Nylon tippets (also called leaders or casts) are the penultimate accoutrement to your basic kit and most nylon made today is relatively cheap but of good quality. I use standard nylon of 4lb (1.8 kg) breaking strain and anything in the 3–6lb (1.4–2.7 kg) range will suffice for the wild loch trout. I usually make the nylon the same length or slightly longer than the rod and advise the novice to use a short rather than very long tippet as that length of nylon is quite enough to control. In very bright, still conditions the nylon will glitter or certainly be more noticeable than in dull windy weather and rubbing the leader with a bit of mud will help though I must confess I sometimes forget to do so. Most disasters with broken nylon or slipped knots are man-made rather than fish-made. If you take more time to check knots and droppers periodically the nylon itself is quite up to the task. One thing I always do is use the nylon cast only once (thus redeeming myself with nylon manufacturers!), as I believe nylon is cheap but my fishing hours will often be priceless and unpicking knots or winding nylon on to cast-holders is largely a waste of that precious angling time. Also nylon develops stress fatigue when it is used several times, perhaps from wind knots or rubbing on stones and therefore storing and re-using old nylon invites lost fish and lost tempers. Keeping nylon spools in strong sunlight also has a similar weakening effect making the nylon brittle and shortening its life considerably. After any angling day it goes without saying that you should take all monofilament home with you and dispose of it safely in the fire or cut it in small pieces into the rubbish bin. Leaving nylon on banks is inexcusable as it has the nasty habit of wrapping itself around any creature that moves causing many unnecessary wildlife deaths each year.

The last but the most important item in your outfit is the fly box (see also Fly-tying, Chapter 7). Throughout Scotland you will find wild trout fly boxes containing an almost infinite variety of flies; some will contain sparsely dressed spider patterns, some only heavily dressed artificials, some will be all wet flies and lure-like dressings, while others are a mix of wet and dry fly, and others still will be predominantly nymph tyings. All these flies will be in a wide selection of sizes anything from size 8 to size 16, with 10s and 12s probably the norm and usually the choice of patterns will be localised to the angler's particular area. You will find that certain flies are favourites in each Scottish county, some would say on each loch! When advising an initial choice of patterns therefore, I give you a broad sweep of successful flies used in Scotland as it would be impossible to detail artificials for each specific region, there are so many and fly choice can be a terribly personal thing!

If I look first at my own fly box I see the colours black, red and brown predominate and nearly all the most successful Scottish loch-style patterns incorporate an element of one of these three colours. Technically this seems to be because the trout see them better than other more pastel shades, but then again is it the outline of the fly or its colour which first stimulates a fish to snatch your artificial, who really knows except a trout?

Soldier Palmer, Black Zulu and Invicta – a deadly trio for Scottish lochs.

I rank my flies as 'prime movers' and 'secondary reserve' with a few specialist numbers kept for specific or difficult occasions:

Amongst the *prime movers* I always have Soldier Palmers, Black or Blue Zulus, Invicta variants and a Ke He or two with the Kate McLaren, Butcher variants (including the Kingfisher Butcher) and the Wickham's Fancy. Bibio, Golden Olive Bumble and Black Pennel are also there.

In the *secondary reserve* you may find the Greenwell's Glory, the Alder Fly, Grouse and Claret, March Brown, Dunkeld, Connemara Black, Blae and Black and others of that ilk.

For *specialist* work I have a selection of (largely hand-tied) dry and wet Daddy-Long-Legs, a few Hare Lug nymphs in soft browns, bushy Loch Ordies, Teal Blue and Silver for the odd sea trout I may encounter, also a fly called the 'Junefly' (tied by the author) which is a heavily dressed pattern rather like a dapping fly, made using those three popular colours of brown, red and black and used during the Highland mayfly season starting in June.

Nearly all my flies are in sizes 10 and 12 but then this is to suit my area where the trout seem always to enjoy a good mouthful. If you are a visitor you should seek local advice on fly size and design for the lochs you are likely to fish. I have found for example that anglers on lowland waters favour much sparser dressed patterns in smaller sizes than my own tyings.

Most of these artificials I fish wet, sub-surface, but there are occasions when I favour making a number of the prime movers dry with a drop of floatant. Any flies with a big hackle or palmered like the Soldier Palmer work very well as dry flies, especially when fish are feeding on the surface.

The extra bounce in these hackled flies makes the fly sit up nicely in the film, something which is usually irresistible to the fish!

Thus armed with the basic tools of the trade there are one or two other items which you *must* have for Scottish loch fishing . . .

Additional Kit

Some form of lightweight waders are essential in the Highlands both for actual shoreline wading and for getting in and out of the boat. This may seem unnecessary advice but I am frequently surprised by the number of visiting anglers we have coming to the far north who expect their fishing to be on a par with the manicured lawn fishings of the south where one simply has to get out of the car and stand on the nearest casting platform to catch trout. Not so here as some wading is usually essential for successful bank fishing in the shallower Scottish lochs. Often you have to go out a long way to be amongst the fish and a landing net is also advised in such situations as walking a fish a long way backward over shallow rocks and weed is asking for it to be lost. The only time wellies can be worn instead of waders is when the loch is very deep off the edge or when the bottom of the loch is soft mud and/or dangerous in some way. Equally you may find you have to heave the boat over several yards of shallows in order to get to the deeper water and thigh waders are necessary for this arduous task. Note: avoid wearing chest waders in boats, they can speed you quickly to the bottom if you fall in and always wear some kind of flotation device when afloat, storms and strong winds can kill quickly in deep exposed lochs. A drogue is an essential tool for slowing down the progress of your drifting boat on the bigger windswept lochs; despite being relatively inexpensive they are often something that many anglers wish they had brought with them but unfortunately do not think about until it is too late and they are being propelled at lightning speed across the loch!

Landing nets are essential for boat fishing and for deep wading when it is a long walk back to the beach, but they are a confounded nuisance if you have a long trek prior to fishing your loch. I must admit if I have the prospect of a lengthy tramp in the heather before fishing the last thing I take with me is a landing net, it just swings irritatingly around and attaches itself like a demonic limpet to any piece of herbage above a foot in height.

Tackle bags for carrying all the fiddly things like boxes, spare jumper, scarf, socks, hat, flask, sandwiches, sunglasses, etc. should again err on the lightweight, you often have to walk a long way with it, and recently I designed a light, multi-purpose rucksack/cum fishing bag which is intended for comfortable walking and practical fishing use. If you have long walks either on the hill or out to the loch, or along the river bank for that matter, then I would recommend trying one of these revolutionary bags which make life so much easier for the avid hill loch or river enthusiast.

Warm and waterproof clothing is always essential especially in Scotland with its fickle weather patterns (see Chapter 8). I use the recommended outdoor-goer's 'layer' system, with a preference for cotton shirts, walking breeches or similar, and perhaps a fleece jacket in summer conditions. In addition to this I also always wear a fishing vest to carry most of those small items for immediate use like snips, priest, fly box, floatant, nylon spools, sunglasses etc. The fishing vest is an indispensable piece of equipment which has more pockets than I know what to do with while acting as an additional layer of insulation. For those heavy showers I take a light but waterproof cagoule with me in the tackle bag perhaps also with a spare jersey if the weather has been unseasonable. Winter conditions (which can happen any time of the year!) demand more layers of clothing and a good covering of thermal underwear is recommended, silk if you can afford it. On cold days I clad myself in numerous thin layers which trap warm air next to the skin and top it off with a waxed jacket, woolly hat and mitts! Dressed in so many layers I may well end up resembling a small Michelin man but it is much easier to take one layer off than risk poor body insulation which, if left untreated, can result in hypothermia. You should also be aware that sitting comparatively still in a boat all day is much colder than walking and wading along the bank and go afloat properly prepared with extra clothing available.

In later summer, midge repellent and/or a midge net worn over the face is vital for sanity when the biting harpies are around. I cannot recommend any brand of midge repellent as better than any other, in some cases nothing at all works, but, if you cover yourself in repellent and don the black mesh net just as you feel the first irritating nip of a midge, you may just be able to keep body and soul intact. I did not start using these nets until about five years ago as I thought them silly, vanity oh vanity, but I have found that though they are not 100 per cent successful and do little to enhance your appearance, they do mean you can keep fishing when all around you have packed up and gone home in disgust!

On more remote Scottish waters a map and compass are important especially if the mist descends either when you are walking or wading or when you are afloat. Even if you are unable to do all the sophisticated things like take bearings and set courses, you can still get a rough idea where north is and relate that to the map to find a rough position. The terrain surrounding isolated hill lochs is remarkably similar with one knobbly rise and bog very like the next. To avoid getting hopelessly lost particularly after a tiring day's fishing when mental faculties are not at their best, it is always advisable to carry at least a compass to help find your way home. If you are caught out in mist it is always better to stay put rather than to try and walk out immediately the hazard descends. Staying put will be cold but you will be safe and the mist may lift comparatively quickly; wandering off in a panic may lead you into dangerous bog or worse off the edge of a precipice – do not laugh and say that would never happen to you because it can and very easily. For hill loch expeditions carrying a whistle is a good safety precaution along with a torch, spare food and one of those 'tin foil' space survival blankets in case you are benighted. Being caught out in mist while afloat on a big expanse of water is even worse because of the total disorientation experienced in this wet grey enveloping blanket which deadens all familiar noises, a distinctly eerie experience. The only way of coping with this I know is to gently drift ashore without the engine running for fear of losing the shear pin and wait for the mist to lift.

Sunscreen protection is needed even on dull days for delicate (and not so delicate) skins which otherwise risk chronic sunburn and/or skin cancer. Sunglasses and a suitable hat are necessary to stop eyes aching after a long day staring at bouncing waves and glittering water. That about completes this list of essentials; let us take a look at what we are going to do with them all . . .

Elementary Casting

Having assembled the appropriate tackle we are ready and, while it is not my intention to teach you how to cast in this book (far too many of the great and good have done this before me in other angling literature), I will proffer some assistance for loch fishing. Though I personally consider the ability to cast a fly as actually only one, albeit necessary, part of the whole gamut of successful loch trouting, I recognise a little adroit assistance for the new-comer would be helpful and, if we cannot meet at the lochside itself to do this, I offer the following hopefully cogent advice through the written medium.

The art of casting a fly is, in the end, only a means of propelling a small piece of fluff and tinsel to a waiting trout in the hope he will be fooled into thinking it is something worthwhile to eat. At its best it is a delightful relaxed form of exercise, rhythmic and skilful, at its worst it is an exhaust-ing, sweaty and frustrating activity from which grown men are known to return fishless and in tears! In any casting on the lochs, keep uppermost in your mind *light touch* and *rhythm* of movement. That basically means that for an overhead cast you have to get the line *up* in the air, letting it stretch out behind you (count 'one, two' as you wait for the line to unfurl if it helps) and then propel it *out* toward the horizon letting the line and its fly come down to rest gently on the water surface. These highlighted words are important, the line goes up in the air not back into the heather, and it goes out over the water rather than crashing down into it. Various instructors will teach the action of casting in differing ways; for example you may hear them refer to casting round an imaginary clock (12 o'clock, 2 o'clock and so on); or they may tell you to think of the rod working as a lever or a spring – you lift the rod and line up with a smooth acceleration, stop when the fly line is fully aerialised, and then send the line lightly back to the water surface crisply with a little flick. The explanation I found the most helpful was to imagine trying to flick an imaginary bit of mud off the end of the rod, an action which propels the line out quite well, and I found visualising that concept a lot more useful than thinking about clocks, springs or levers, but then I am not very mechanical! It will help if you remember to straighten your back, relax, tuck your elbows in and let the rod do the work as you lift the line off the water. I sometimes see novices casting as if they are trying to throw a lead brick at the water putting every bit of effort into throwing line, rod and body weight at the loch, often bending forward and giving themselves the first stages of lumbago as well. Resist the urge to try and follow your fly into the depths for you are actually shortening the length of the cast not prolonging it. Much more distance is achieved by letting the rod propel the fly with your body staying in a reasonably upright stance – osteopaths' bills are also halved! If you are a complete novice therefore, I would urge you to get some rudimentary practical casting instruction first, rather than teaching yourself awkward and often unnecessarily tiring habits.

Actions for casting flies from the boat or the bank are quite similar though when sitting down I usually have to raise my casting arm up higher, away from my body, than I would do on the bank to achieve the same length of line; perhaps I am so small I need more clearance over the edge of the boat! 'Overhead' casting and an ability to 'roll' cast (when the line is cast in such a way as to avoid background obstructions, rolling it out in a large loop rather than lifting it up overhead) can usually be mastered in one or two lessons with an experienced instructor and it will pay you dividends in time and temper to develop an initially sound technique.

For the more experienced, I would urge some caution in applying lovely casting skills learnt on manicured stillwaters (often sheltered kindly from the elements) to wild windswept Highland lochs. Endlessly struggling to cast against a blasting bitter wind can make your delightfully refined technique superfluous as you struggle even to stand upright. Scottish conditions can play havoc even with the best of casting personas, but that is all part of the fun not to say the challenge! Note also that lots of swishing and/or false casting is not usually necessary for the length of line needed for loch fishing is often quite short. We should be casting to where the fish are after all and not purely for the sake of showy long lines.

Loch fly fishing on Orkney is quaintly referred to as 'wafting the wand' and that is a lovely description of what it should be, not wielding a pickaxe but wafting a gentle wand. Bear in mind that while being able to cast is important, you have to be able to reach the trouts lies after all, most highly successful anglers for loch trout follow quite basic casting methods; where they excel is in their practical knowledge of the wild trout and its habitat. Strive therefore for reasonable accuracy and delicacy in propelling fly and fly line around but balance your efforts by remembering that the final judge of your skills is solely a wild and wily fish. 'Tammy Troot' is not going to award you extra accolades because you managed to cast twenty-five yards instead of fifteen, in fact he will not even notice unless you happen to land a suitable artificial on his snout. Nor is he going to laugh at your efforts if flies are caught up in heather or cracked off on stones, well not much anyway! Loch fishing for wild trout is about watercraft, knowing where the fish are and what they are likely to feed on, just as much if not more so than looking good with a piece of carbon fibre.

Wading

It is often assumed that to be successful in loch-style fishing you must have the use of a boat when in fact careful bank fishing, forearmed with the knowledge I have already imparted on assessing the loch as a whole, will bring just as many fish to your basket. If you are a complete beginner at fishing for wild trout, or an angler exclusively versed in rainbow trout fishing, I would always recommend starting this great and enjoyable learning process of fishing for loch trout from the bank. When you are worrying about wobbling boats, losing oars, snapping off shear pins and running out of fuel you cannot possibly do your fishing justice. Start on the bank and be done with it.

Wading is personally my favourite form of loch fishing, I just love being in the watery element, stalking trout, moving steadily along the shore covering new trout lies, often accompanied unseen by my fellow hunters the otter, the heron and the diver. While I am doing so I can learn so much not only of fish behaviour but also of the natural world as a whole. Rarely do I return from a loch without learning at least one new snippet of knowledge, even if it is a water I have fished many times before. It could be the thrill of seeing that first hatch of sedge emanating from the shore after a long winter, something which I know will stir the trout into action, or possibly the discovery of an otter spraint or the first frog spawn or stickleback fry of the year. Wading is a solitary, thoughtful game largely engaged in watery silence but spiced by the occasional thrill of a trout suddenly engulfing the fly. Senses become sharply honed and your hearing seems more acute as you concentrate on listening for the splash or deep swirling gloop of a heavy fish. There is the chance to contemplate and to absorb in silence. In a boat you can also do this but for me it is annoyingly more distracting having to row, keep the boat on the drift, fiddle with engines and so on. Wading is unencumbered with the tools, accoutrements and machinery of water transport and its effects are much more relaxing, concentrating the mind like no other exercise I know.

There is a lovely natural rhythm to this kind of fishing, a cast to the big rock here, a turn over on the skerries (partly submerged rocks and boulders) there, as you wade at your own pace in zigzag fashion along the shore. A word of caution is to always move in and out of the shore as you travel along it seeking the fish, wading straight out to deeper water and then trying to move along parallel to the bank can mean you get into severe difficulties with soft mud patches or sudden holes, so zigzag for safety at all times. Lochs with lily beds, muddy bottoms or very deep drops straight from the edge should not be waded for obvious reasons and occasionally local rules will stipulate you must use the boat rather than bank fish so do follow any local advice given. Wading around a loch in a day you can cover some distance, often a couple of miles or more, and you will end up a long way from where you began but then that is a small price to pay for such enjoyment in exploring new bays, weed beds, skerries, old walls, fences and all the other territories harbouring trout. For the wader so engaged, around every corner there is always 'one more cast' and for a time all cares are forgotten.

Successful wading!

Early season, with the fish sheltering well inshore, thigh waders or even wellies are sufficient to cover most of the trout in the shallows, indeed they are often only feet from the bank. Later in the summer months of July and August I will use chest waders as the larger more cautious fish will have 'flitted' offshore to deeper, safer shelter. Wading should be undertaken with some stealth remembering that although fish hear nothing outwith their watery habitat they certainly sense some vibration noise within it; clodhopping around in shallow feeding margins will achieve little other than putting all the fish down in the immediate vicinity.

It is vitally important to wade along the shore at a pace as fast as the drifting boat, standing still in one spot will only cover the possible trout lies immediately in front of you and they will soon be exhausted. Constantly seek out new fish territories with a steady rhythmic tempo and try only two or three casts of different lengths at the one spot before moving down a few paces. Take only small steps, feeling with your feet for any obstructions liable to trip you up and it goes without saying you should always wade with some caution if you are unfamiliar with a loch shoreline as sudden drop-offs can lead to unexpected duckings or worse. I am such a cautious old stick now that I rarely wade in water deeper than about my hips and if I cannot see the bottom of an unknown loch I am loath to take any unnecessary risks. Happily, with wading undertaken at a gentle unhurried pace, very few accidents occur. It is usually only with thoughtless action executed in haste (often when that big trout suddenly rises that bit further away) that unexpected contact with cold water is made! Note that when the going underfoot is slimy rock, especially that deadly green stringy algae, I have found that boots with metal studs are really the only answer. Felt soles will cope with this hazard initially, but they wear down after a year or so, and also have the embarrassing quality of tipping you on your backside immediately you come out of the water on to wet grass or peat. Cleated rubber soles also wear down quite quickly to nasty bald patches though admittedly they are easier to walk any distance in.

Boat anglers are sometimes critical of wading as something which disturbs the trout and his invertebrate food in the shallows and this is quite correct if it is done heavy-handedly. However, undertaken with lightness of step and a degree of judgement as to where the fish are likely to be according to the time of year, it will often bring many more trout to the angler's rod. Wading gives you time to return to that exact spot where you saw the big trout rise having rested it say for half an hour; in a boat drifting fast in the gale you get no second attempt and marking the correct place where a good rise occurred is very difficult if not impossible. On most lochs the trout are lying adjacent to their larder and their safe houses, roughly around where the shallow water begins to deepen, and judicious wading will usually cover most of their lies; remember that boat anglers are nearly always casting toward the shoreline and bank anglers are casting out toward the boats! Bank technique is obviously affected by the prevailing weather conditions and flat calms, with your every movement obvious, can call for much slower walking when wading. Good ripples with little or no sunshine are best and mean you can cover a lot more ground with your intentions easily disguised by wind and wave.

Wading where safely permitted, is for me the simplest yet most enjoyable form of wild trout fishing. It is fishing and walking in time with the elements when the only distractions are the call of the wild geese or the splash and grab of a hungry trout – wonderful stuff!

Boating

Loch style and boats 'gang thegither' and many wild trout anglers would never dream of going on the loch without a boat. By going afloat they gain considerable advantage in being able to cover much more water than the bank fisher and also have a welcome chance to sit down and fish rather than having to keep walking to new trout territories. Traditionally loch-style fishing has virtually always been executed afloat. W. C. Stewart, in 1857, refers to the angler and his boatman (gillie) on trout lochs and this convention, set in the nineteenth century, still has great popularity, though nowadays few can consistently afford the luxuries of a strong-armed boatman to manoeuvre their craft and place them over the best fishing areas. Any boating offers a wonderful escape from terra firma and can be a real joy with a good companion to share the day's experiences. Gentle drifts on a June evening amidst rising trout with the water softly lapping the side of the boat are a positive delight and you can travel in relatively relaxed fashion over much longer distances unencumbered by having to walk over difficult terrain in heavy waders.

There are a few basic pointers, however, I can offer the novice or visitor when using a boat, particularly one which is on hire. First, make sure the craft is water worthy: there are no obvious leaks and the bung, baler and painter (rope for tying up the boat) are there along with the rowlocks and the oars. A drogue to slow down very fast progress in windy weather is also a must (you will usually have to provide it yourself) and wear a flotation device on all Scottish lochs; yes I know many do not, but falling into icy cold water in heavy waders and waxed jackets can kill much quicker than you would imagine. A cushion of some sort to sit on is very necessary if you are going afloat for the day, not to take one may render you unable to sit down anywhere else for the rest of the week! If an engine is allowed on the loch, some do not permit it, make sure you have spare fuel, spare shear pin and that the beast does operate with some precision before you start off!

Frequently I have watched from the comfort of the bank as frantic attempts are made to start a temperamental engine with the boat drifting perilously close to the rocks, such efforts usually being accompanied by streams of abuse and a mad scrambling for oars to fend off the impending collision! A landing net is vital to lift your catch into the boat, small fish can be unceremoniously hauled over the side but good trout invariably fall off so take it with you. Spare tackle is also useful and extra warm, water-proof clothing is essential if you are travelling over a large exposed expanse of water.

This advice may sound somewhat rudimentary but you would be very surprised how many in their rush to get afloat do not bother to check such simple details and they wish they had done so prior to reaching the middle of a windswept loch.

In boats, safety is always more uppermost in my mind than when on the bank, but then perhaps I am not now the best of sailors, somehow along the way the recklessness of youth has been replaced with a more cautious outlook, boring I know, but safer! Before going afloat it will pay you to determine if possible, any dangerous boating areas to avoid, for example underwater boulders which can hole your boat, and also how best to navigate the loch particularly if it is large and you have to travel over a big expanse of water to reach the fishing grounds. When leaving your boat anchorage head up into the wind with the object of drifting back down the loch using the wind power to assist your drift direction. Carefully avoid disturbing other anglers using the bank or boats; cutting across other's drifts or wading areas is not *de rigueur* and can appear downright rude. Sadly such irritations are still caused on many waters by anglers deter-mined to reach their drift by the quickest possible means to the detriment of other water users. If the wind is strong hug the shoreline for better protection and quicker progress and then, once reaching a suitable fishing point, for example round the edge of a promontory or the neck of a bay, switch off the engine, lift the propeller upward to avoid damaging it on shallow rocks, turn the boat broadside and drift down with wind behind you. Use the drogue to slow down your progress if you are going too fast and fish back to your starting point to your heart's content. Physically controlling the boat, also known as 'holding drift', is not quite as easy as it looks, use the oars to keep the boat at right angles to the wind and to help keep the drift on line. Novices to boat fishing will find this quite tiresome at first especially if the boat is of light construction and liable to annoyingly swing off beam at the vital moment, usually just as a big trout sticks his neb up for the only rise of his day!

In the boat you should be aiming to keep your artificial flies over the trout's territories, for example at the edges of weed beds or skerries, and keeping over the shallower feeding areas is almost always more productive than drifting over deep icy water. Unless the loch is uniformly shallow, when you will be able to fish more or less anywhere, most boat anglers can be seen casting flies toward the bank and drifting into or along parallel with the shore, normally over water anything between 4 and 10ft (1.2 and 3m) deep. If you are drifting along parallel with the shore, remember to vary the line of drift slightly by using an oar to push the boat in and out of the margins thereby covering trout habitats at a number of different depths. Underwater features providing bolt-holes for the fish are not found at a constant twenty yards from the shore, in fact they will vary considerably in position, so drift in and out to cover all those sub-surface trout lies. If your line of drift takes this fact into account many more fish are likely to be raised than if you proceed in a monotonous straight line.

Look out for the formation of wind lanes, lines of scummy water with the appearance of a slightly flatter surface than the rest of the waves. This is a natural phenomenon occurring on most lochs during windy weather and often the lanes hold dross tossed up from the shallows or blown in from the bank. This dross contains invertebrate and microscopic life the trout will always enjoy and therefore casting into and across wind lanes is always a worthwhile exercise.

Weather conditions, particularly gales and/or heavy rain, have considerably more influence on boat anglers than those on the calmer banks. Scottish weather is extremely fickle (see Chapter 8) and out on the bigger lochs you are very exposed not to say highly vulnerable to strong winds. If you are confident you will enjoy being tossed around like a cork and believe in your ability to manoeuvre boats and operate engines in such conditions, then gale fishing is still a possibility and sometimes good fish will rise with vigour during rough conditions. I am now such an abject coward in bad weather I rarely venture out afloat in it unless wearing two lifejackets and chewing on valium, but nevertheless I do see hardened local anglers standing up in their boats, happily casting away in what appears a force nine gale! Standing up in any craft is not advised though I understand from anglers so engaged that the reasoning behind it is the ability to throw a longer line and also to control the boat better when manoeuvring it. The latter theory may well be true but regarding the length of line I would have thought the boat is actually capable of doing much of the distance work for you – if you want to cover a fish territory all you need to do is drift or row toward it. My only honest reason for standing up in a boat is to relieve the pain of a numbed backside because I inadvertently forgot my cushion!

If you have gone afloat in good conditions and the weather suddenly begins to deteriorate how do you know when to stop fishing and turn tail? I would suggest from years of experiencing wild conditions that it is when you are no longer enjoying the experience, cannot hear what your partner is saying though he may be only two feet away and when the water takes on that spattered appearance of 'cats' paws'. These cats' paws occur when the wind is buffeting down on the water as well as across it and will make any presentation of your fly almost impossible. The water appears to break up in spatters and great swirls appear on the loch when viewed from above. If you are caught out by such adverse winds which are becoming dangerous I can only advise motoring, drifting or rowing into the side; it may be a long walk back but at least you will be safe on dry land. If you have to run for cover avoid turning on the engine and heading straight down wind as you start to slop in water over the back of the boat and can flounder. Shipping in water, in any circumstances, is a sign to get off the loch as quickly as possible even if this means going straight into the side rather than heading back to the harbour.

Practised sensibly, boating is pleasurable and great fun allowing much more freedom of movement around the loch but safety should always be a priority and remember that discretion in really bad weather is always the better part of valour.

6
Loch-Style Techniques I

They know enough who know how to learn.

HENRY ADAMS

Wet-Fly Loch Fishing

The use of a team of wet flies, that is flies that are cast out, allowed to sink, then drawn back to the angler beneath the water surface, is undoubtedly the most traditional and widely used form of loch-style fishing. Generations of trout loch anglers have grown up using this method and it still remains the most popular and successful on Scottish lochs today. As far back as the early to mid-nineteenth century, 'wet fly' on lochs has always meant using several flies rather than just the one. W. C. Stewart mentions using a considerable number of patterns, anything between three and twelve in number, placed along a gut cast at a distance of about 2ft (60 cm) apart. Twelve flies must have been quite a handful to manipulate successfully on a windswept water and today I have personally not encountered anglers using more than four flies to a cast. The norm in my Highland area is three flies or less and this tradition is now widespread in Scotland. The original idea behind using several patterns, rather than just one fly, was to give the angler several chances to attract a trout, quite literally covering all possibilities in fact. It was widely thought that using only one fly would catch less trout than several tempting morsels fished at different depths and today most wet-fly loch fishers continue to follow this concept.

In wet-fly boat fishing for wild loch trout, teams of flies tied dropper fashion on nylon of (normally) 4lb BS (1.8 kg) are fished with a traditional floating line or occasionally an intermediate line. The nylon is at least as long as the rod used and the droppers should be spaced out to around 3ft (90 cm) apart, more if you can manage it. Usually a bushy fly is used for the top dropper so that it trips well over the surface as the retrieve of the team is completed; the rest of the flies are personal selections according to what is happening on the day. Sinking lines can also be used in wet-fly fishing but I personally do not find they are as enjoyable to use – all that keel hauling up from the depths is too much like hard work – but if you think the trout are lying at some considerable depth by all means give a 'sinker' a whirl. In modern Scottish competition fishing there is much store placed on changing the line frequently to reach fish at different depths even when using traditional wet fly. I am assured that changing lines is necessary to get amongst the trout quickly; speed is essential in say a one-day competition, but in my more leisurely days on hill lochs if I want my fly to fish deeper I simply still use the floating line but let the flies sink well (counting to twenty helps) before retrieving them back. Perhaps this is laziness but it works well enough for my own needs and fits in with my local brown trout's environment where fish are rarely found in deep, icy cold water. In less pressured wet-fly 'top of the water' fishing floating lines are still the accepted norm therefore, and the technique used from the boat involves the active use of the lighter density line to 'work' the top dropper of the cast, trickling it on the water surface before lifting off to recast elsewhere. Although droppers can also be worked off the bank, somehow it does not seem quite so successful a technique as when afloat. Wet-fly skills are used throughout the season March to October, and as much as 90 per cent of the Scottish wild trout angler's time will be spent using wet fly on the lochs, indeed some never use anything else!

In the boat you will see experienced anglers cast out their wet fly team with floating line; casting distances vary but short lines about fifteen yards or so work well and then, once the flies settle and drop below the surface, they draw them back to the boat with the rod parallel to the water. There is a

Traditional loch-style may be practised from the boat or the bank. Loch Hakel, Tongue, Sutherland.

tension on the line so that the angler keeps good contact with his flies and the retrieve will normally be at a sympathetic, medium pace giving the flies a pulsing life without stripping them willy-nilly through the water. Just before they make another cast you should see them lift the rod tip to bring the top dropper to bob on the surface, something which usually works exceptionally well in attracting trout up from below. Even if the top dropper is not taken the trout may well have come up to look at your 'attractor' and then turn down on your sub-surface point fly engulfing it instead. I personally favour only two flies for wet-fly boat work, having given up on unpicking annoying fankled droppers, and space them about 5–6ft (1.5–1.8m) apart on a leader of around 11ft (3.4m) which allows the flies to do their separate jobs both at depth and on the surface. A slimline fly for the point and a nice bushy attractor like the Soldier Palmer or a Zulu variant for the top dropper would be typical examples of the make-up of the cast. The flies are deliberately dissimilar in shape and outline and the streamlined point fly is meant to search the depths as a general representation perhaps of a small fish fry while the bushy bob fly imitates a wide range of insects nearer the top of the water. I place great store on keeping the droppers well spaced out so that even if a trout is put off by my first offering it will perceive the second one as something unrelated to it and may well chew on that instead. I usually change the fly every fifteen minutes or so if they fail to meet with success and I vary the speed of retrieve according to what artificials are used. For example a nymph-like point fly may require a slow retrieve to imitate its lengthy passage to the surface or a quicker, darting retrieve may be necessary for a Butcher to imitate the movement of a small fish fry.

One of many experiences epitomising good wet-fly fishing from the boat was time spent on Loch Harray in Orkney with local fisher Ed Headley. Harray is renowned as one of the principal lochs in northern Scotland for traditional wet-fly fishing and short lining from the boat working the bob fly on the surface is the norm here. Conditions had been cruelly bright for most of my week but finally the last day saw a good grey sky, nice wave and plenty of insect activity. We plied the teams of wets around the shallow, weedy skerries of Harray, a drift here, a rise there, lovely dreamy fishing for Orkney has such enormous vistas from its flat lands and the sky seems so big it would swallow you up. In Merkister bay I had a good fish of 1lb 8oz (685g) to a Red Invicta but Ed topped that with one of 1lb 12oz (800g) to his own hand-tied Orange Invicta. The chat was happy, the fish rose superbly and the day ended with a glass of Ed's wonderful home-made fruit wine at his home in Finstown. Such is the stuff of great days with the wet fly from the boat, treasured memories.

Fishing wet fly from the bank I will normally employ similar floating line tactics while wading, casting and retrieving flies over where I think the trout are lying with that medium-paced retrieve occasionally slowing it down for extra depth or speeding it up, but I have never found fast lure stripping of much success nor do I favour a crawling 'figure of eight' retrieve which I find too slow in any wave. I keep the rod parallel to the water when retrieving and have the fly line virtually straight to keep in constant touch with my artificials as they search through and under the waves. This method also allows for a good striking action, trying to attract a quicksilver wild fish with the rod wavering skyward and a loop of loose line between you and the fish gives you considerably less chance of firmly hooking anything. It was pointed out to me recently that in fact my line does not always lie completely straight out across the water for there is some-what of an arc introduced by my wading along while leaving it in place on the loch. Thus when I do begin the actual retrieve the fly swings round slightly in a curve for I have actually moved my body position by several feet. I must admit that I had never really given this much thought but now that I consider it I have noticed some good fish taking hold after I have let the fly sink, waded along and then started the retrieve. The fish just seem suddenly to be there without warning as the fly swings back toward me in that very slight curve. Whether unconsciously using this slight crescent line method, by walking and fishing at the same time, is more proficient in attracting trout I cannot really say but I do know with certainty that I catch many more wild trout by keeping the rod tip parallel with the water and a tension on the fly line, arcs or no arcs! Because I want constant contact with what is going on sub-surface I do not tend to work the top dropper as often as when in the boat as this means having to raise that rod tip and create some slack line, something I am rather loath to do off the bank. However this is my own foible and I know of others more expert than I who can work top droppers while wading with just as much success as afloat, so try it yourself and see.

Wet-fly bank fishing is at its most effective when flies are cast across the wind and trout facing 'upstream' into it are shown the whole outline of the fly rather than just its hook end. If the wind is directly behind the angler, the line may go further but the fish takes can be more difficult to secure as the trout will sometimes just pluck at the fly and be off again. By keeping the fly line straight (or arced!) out across the waves I keep in touch with the moving flies drawing them temptingly over the noses of any upwind feeding fish. I know for the novice casting across the wind is more difficult, but great distance is not required to be over the trout as they seem more assured about holding station quite close inshore and will take your artificial confidently in the right conditions. Just as in the boat, takes with wet fly usually occur beneath or just on the surface varying from the most gentle of plucks to a good arm-wrenching tweak but any kind of 'pull' should immediately be met with a pull back by lifting the rod tip to put a taut line between you and the prospective fish. When fishing across the wind the fish often effectively hook themselves, if fishing with the wind directly behind they seem more cautious and I personally lose more trout this way, but perhaps this is my misfortune and not others. I rarely strike a fish hard – lifting into the weight of the fish firmly but not with a wrench is usually enough, I want to hook him not break his jaw! The trout should be played out in the normal way keeping the rod vertical and the line taut and once the fish raises his head and/or turns on his side he is ready for the net or to be beached.

I do differ from most wet-fly enthusiasts in that often I use only one fly from the bank, changing it every ten to fifteen minutes until one proves successful. This habit started because I nearly always seemed to catch the bigger trout on the point fly making the others superfluous and also while fishing in the northern Highlands I have had to endure some quite appallingly rough cold weather suffering ghastly experiences with frozen fingers and tangled nylon; in the end one speedily changed fly just seemed a lot more sensible!

It is no secret I prefer to 'specimen hunt' rather than catch numerous small fish which I would normally return, and if fishing an unfamiliar loch I have a trio of Size 10 'wets' which are employed singly in a particular order using a floating line and medium-paced retrieve. I have a firm belief in the theory that lots of flies crashing down in a heap attract less fish than one neatly placed artificial and I will normally start with a lone black Zulu, for black and red are usually the most effective colours for most Scottish lochs. Of all loch flies the Zulu is probably one of the most deadly, something to do with its outline and colour which always seems to stimulate aggression. If that does not attract even a faint splutter I take it off and put on the Soldier Palmer, brown and red and whiskery, a seductive pulsing fly which bears more than a passing resemblance to the freshwater shrimp but also serves as a general representation of most struggling insects. If there is still no response next in line is an Invicta. The Invicta is a strange fly much favoured as a sedge imitation but also doing business as a small darting fish fry if retrieved quickly through the waves.

Eventually one of these traditional patterns will usually find success provided I am over the correct trout territories, fish are actively feeding and the weather is reasonably mild and overcast. They are, of course, my personal 'big three' flies, other loch anglers may never use them at all. Fly choice on lochs can be psychological as much as realistic, but over numerous years these have been found to be my most productive on most Scottish lochs. I do give some variation to their traditional dressings, however, if I can find enough time to hand-tie them, and like to produce common, and not so common, variants of these great conventional patterns. For example an Orange Invicta (traditional) may go on to do the business when the yellow blue-throated one fails, or a bushy Zulu with a green or orange tail (non-traditional as far as I am aware) instead of a red one, might also be more effective. The Golden Olive Bumble (traditional), a very effective fly I have started using only fairly recently, more's the pity, has its coloration rooted in the Invicta dressing, rather resembling a hackled Invicta without its wing, and it is well worth tying up when sedge or cow dung fly are on the water. Sometimes fly shape is enough to attract trout sub-surface, sometimes it has more to do with its movement in the water, but that is all part of the intrigue of wet-fly fishing!

If for some reason all of these flies fail from the bank but I am still convinced fish are moving sub-surface, then I would rethink tactics perhaps changing my line to an intermediate one for more depth and plump next for flies like the Kate McLaren, Butcher, Ke He, Pennel or Bibio again fished singly. I nearly always use most of my prime movers first before switching to a pattern in the secondary reserve or an obtuse specialist number (see Chapter 5). Most of my choices are amongst the stalwart patterns of wet-fly fishing but whatever artificial is selected eventual success in wet-fly fishing will accrue from your watercraft skills and powers of observation and yes, just a modicum of luck in being in the right place at the right time!

It is impossible for me to give you a perfect example of bank wet-fly fishing, there have been different and challenging experiences, but if I can recommend one loch where I ply this craft frequently it would be Loch Calder in Caithness, a personal favourite. I firmly believe if you want to experience traditional 'wets from the bank' there are few waters to beat dusky, windy, dramatic Calder. Technically you could term this loch a reservoir as it supplies the water for the nearby town of Thurso but it has little similarity with the big dams of the south, in fact the dam is tucked off in a small bay and is hardly a noticeable feature. The shores have wonderful little microenvironments of marl, sandstone, boulders, peat, weed and gravel and whilst bank fishing it is possible for me to cover a goodly range of trout habitats within 500 yards or so of walking. Though mainly I raise half pounders to the single wet (usually a Zulu or a Soldier Palmer) there is always the possibility of something much bigger hitting the fly and my best from the bank here was 3lb 2oz (2kg) (a stickleback-feeder in August). Fishing wets on Calder with the wail of the diver, the cackle of geese or the splash of an otter is the essence of traditional wet fly and fishing there always leaves me wanting more.

Any visiting angler to our lochs should be able to learn much from the expert traditional wet-fly man just by watching his techniques for a moment either from the boat or the bank. There is a calm intensity to his movements as he methodically sinks those flies and then draws them back pulsing with life through and beneath the waves. His vision is focused out over the water to where the flies are, looking for any unusual movement, break or swirl in the surface, and note how intently he listens for the sound of a moving fish. Mind and body are concentrated as he works those artificials, always aware of where they are and he keeps a tension on the line feeling for that exciting pluck of a hungry trout. He appears content, undistracted and at peace. Strive to be like him or her, the hunter on the shore or the intent figure hunched in the drifting boat.

Dry Fly on Lochs

'The dry fly has been advocated as useful in lochs. Of this plan we have but little experience and that far from encouraging.' So wrote the distinguished trio of 'Three Anglers' in their book *How to Catch Trout* (1888). Their thinking just about sums up the theory passed from generation to generation that dry fly has no real place amongst the pounding waves of Scottish lochs. This widespread historical assumption, rarely contradicted except perhaps by noted anglers such as Bridgett in the 1930s, was a great pity for it had the effect of somewhat lessening the modern interest in what is a fascinating and exciting branch of our sport. At certain times of the wild trout season, dry fly will work just as well on lochs as it does the rolling stream or river and there are many occasions out on the big waters when wet fly simply will not do the business and the 'dry' comes into its own.

I use dry fly exclusively on a floating line, normally in the months of June, July and August, but also at any time when trout are vigorously feeding right on the surface. Frequently I have had the experience of a prolific hatch of insect beginning on hill lochs while I have been fishing the traditional wet fly and as if by magic the trout suddenly and exasperatingly start to ignore my previously successful wet-fly tactics but will avidly snatch the same fly if it is made dry with a dab of floatant. Note I say the same fly for it is not necessary to go to the expense of buying a whole new range of up-eyed 'dry' flies, simply making dry the ones you already have will usually prove successful as well as saving you a penny or two. Dry Ke Hes and dry Zulus are two of my favourites when the fish are up and active on the surface and the slashing vigour with which the trout take these invariably sets the adrenalin flowing. Conversely in any very dour conditions where the loch appears totally dead, the use of a Size 10 dry Daddy-Long-Legs or French Partridge can spectacularly move fish when all else has failed, though be warned, you do not always hook them!

There are other conditions, apart from profuse insect hatches or 'dead' days on the loch, when the dry fly is extremely deadly. During an angling day you can run up against a whole gamut of weather variations, and flat calms are actually not uncommon, particularly after a strong westerly gale blows itself to a standstill. The technique for dry fly on still loch conditions is not very difficult, simply cast out as delicately as you can your chosen well 'ginked' fly and leave it static for a while. If nothing takes an interest start a slow retrieve contrasted with an occasional twitch to make things more lifelike while keeping the rod parallel with the water. Using small modern Mini Muddlers or Hoppers like this makes them look all the world like a struggling sedge or moth and these look extraordinarily lifelike both to angler and fish and prove extremely effective in dusk light. Do not take your eyes off that fly for a moment because even if nothing appears to be happening it may well do so in a violent split second and I speak with some experience when I say that inattention leads to lost trout! If you do attract a fish you will normally not see the follow unless perhaps a fin breaks the surface, all you usually see is a sudden eruption in the water as a bar of gold rips up from the depths, slaps down on your fly and disappears with it clenched in its jaws. Your immediate reaction is normally a) to involuntarily jump; and b) to quickly strike in time-honoured fashion. Overly fast striking however, only succeeds in jerking the fly away from the trout's mouth, instead give him time to porpoise over and turn down on the fly before placing tension on the line in the usual way. Occasionally all the trout will do is knock the fly down underwater sometimes smacking it dramatically with their tails, and then go on to take it at leisure sub-surface. This is more difficult to judge and I would advise as in all loch fishing to keep contact between you and the fly, wait for him, feel for that pull and then lift into the fish. If you do not connect, try a cast again in the immediate vicinity, but if a second attempt fails rest the area, mentally marking the spot as a good trout territory and return to it either later in the day or on another occasion.

Many bigger trout of a pound or over often go for the dry fly when your more exact wet representations have failed *but* if they do not hook themselves first time and become aware of the artificial's deadly intent, they rarely rise again to it, or any other method, that day. I suppose they have grown big from cunning and caution and seem to have some capability of memory, particularly fear. Frost and Brown in *The Trout* refer to the trout's ability to retain some memory and since fear is the strongest emotion, even in fish, it does seem likely.

Nevertheless some of my best wild browns have come to the dry fly and I would never hesitate to use it from May to the end of the season. Dry fly can also be combined with wet by using a wet imitation on the sunk point of the cast and a nice dry attractor on the bob fly again worked from the floating line. I have met a number of expert anglers who favour this method particularly mid-season when fish are actively feeding at different depths in the loch. The only time I can say with some certainty that a dry fly will not work is usually very early or very late in the season when air and water temperatures are at their coldest effectively stopping any surface fish activity; however there will always be one trout to prove me wrong.

Finishing a tucked blood knot for a dry 'Loch Ordie'.

I recall with particular relish an excruciatingly difficult day on one of the clearwater Storr lochs on the island of Skye. I had walked miles, plied every team of wets imaginable, got soaked and gale-blasted, seen only one good fish, had frustrating plucks and lost several trout, and as time was pressing, I shouldered the rod and began walking disconsolately back to the car. As I rounded a little bay the wind dropped quite suddenly and a hatch of small sedges fluttered out from the bank. A good fish rose quite some way out and I cast half-heartedly at it, nothing. I walked a little further down and cast again with a Connemara Black I believe, no not interested. 'Dry Fly,' a little voice said in the corner of my now extremely tired brain and I took off the Connemara and replaced it with a dry Wickham's. I was so exhausted with struggling against wind and rain I could not even manage a well-placed cast and the Wickham's fell well short of where I thought the trout was lying. In a flash a great neb appeared and rolled over, sucking down the fly in the scissors. I struck and a weighty exquisitely marked 2lb 12oz fish (1.25kg) was eventually beached precariously after a furious tumultuous battle in the clear waters of the Storr lochs. As I bore the fish back the spring returned to my step and all exhaustion vanished, what joy with a dry fly – happy days!

Never underestimate the intriguing use of the dry fly on Scottish lochs, not only is it highly exciting and a delight to use, its capabilities in overcoming adverse conditions are quite legion and I would urge you strongly to get out the gink and give it a go!

Nymphing

I used to do a lot of nymph fishing by wading the shallows early on in the season and found it a particularly useful technique when I could see no surface activity from the wild trout of my local Highland lochs. However, while it is true I have taken some good trout in the 2lb (1kg) class by this slower, almost ponderous, method it is not my most favoured, but that is not to decry it as a good tactic to try when the occasion demands. The technique for using nymphs on lochs is very similar to wet fly on intermediate or sinking line, except the retrieve should be much slower to allow that sink and draw of the fly to imitate a small insect rising slowly up to the water surface and then struggling to emerge from its nymph 'shuck' or case as a flying insect. In some ways nymph fishing is a much more exact form of imitative loch angling, unfortunately the terms 'nymph' and 'nymphing' have got rather enmeshed with rainbow trout reservoir techniques and confusion is sometimes the result. Every year in the Highlands I encounter visiting anglers using their hefty, bulbous multi-coloured rainbow trout 'nymphs' with little or no success. It does seem that while traditional flies can make the transition to stillwaters, the opposite is not the case and the canny Scottish trout tends to studiously ignore any alien offerings!

In actual fact the concept of using nymphs on wild Scottish lochs is not new and a considerable number of the old traditional flies have their original roots in nymphal forms. The famous Scottish angler of the 1920s and 30s, R. C. Bridgett, designed a number of spidery patterns which he said were to represent nymphs including one of his own, the 'Black Nymph', which bears more than a passing resemblance to a sparse Pennel or Black Spider, except the hackle is speckled guinea-fowl, and this he recommended as very effective early in the season. Following on from Bridgett's thinking it can also be supposed that many of the sparser dressed wet flies are taken by trout as nymphs. So it would seem that many old and modern wet-fly anglers using a sparsely dressed dark wingless fly on their three-fly cast, are at the same time fishing nymph imitations, though they would not immediately class themselves as enthusiasts of nymph fishing.

Apart from spidery imitations other successful nymph patterns include that very old pattern the Gold Ribbed Hare's Ear also known in Scotland as the Hare Lug. This is a highly versatile nymph pattern, tied without wings and is of particular use when any olives are emerging on the loch, usually from April on. It also happens to be the most successful nymph pattern I have used so it does command some respect in my box! At one time, when very enthusiastic about using this technique, I tied numerous Hare Lug variants with little dashes of orange or yellow seal's fur at the head of the normally dark brown hairy body of the fly, occasionally also adding a very thin wing of starling feather as in the dressing described in Tom Stewart's *Two Hundred Popular Flies*. I recall the orange-headed Hare Lug was the most successful (with or without the wing) when used singly or in twos, sunk on a long leader on either a floating or an intermediate line and then slowly drawn back toward me with a languid retrieve. They worked with dramatic effect on Loch Loyal, a noted brown trout loch in the northern half of Sutherland, when I fished there very early in the season with the lambing snows of April still on the peaks of Ben Stuminadh and Ben Loyal. My family had wandered off walking up toward the slopes of Stuminadh and I was wading alone in a very clear-watered bay. The conditions were very bright but cool with a tang of frost and such weather I would not normally associate with good fishing, but I had an hour to spare so why not! I saw no surface activity anywhere and even when a small hatch of olive appeared not a fish showed. I had already tried my favourite wets without success and put on my orangey-headed Hare Lug as a change of tactic though inwardly I did not envisage any success with it (such positive thinking!). However as nymphing gives me a chance to slow down and day-dream as much as anything it was a welcome respite and I recall watching my little son's red wellingtons appear and disappear as he hopped and skipped along the beach of the far bank. It was lovely even if I was not catching anything but quite unexpectedly I did make contact with an excellent overwintered fish which screamed around the little bay and when beached was a superb 1lb 12oz (800g) specimen making very good eating for all the family, not least the hungry hill-walkers!

Though I have caught large, beautiful overwintered browns with this painstaking technique I also recall that after two seasons of using nymphs in March and April I stopped. Why? Well it had something to do with the fact that early season nymphing with its slower drawing retrieve keeping the fly deep is a very lengthy affair and I am just not one for standing relatively still numbed to the bone with icy north winds blowing down my neck. Also I found that though eventually I might catch a solid overwintered fish by this method the time taken to do so was protracted and frankly a bit tiresome. Eventually I totted up a few statistics and found the early season catch figures were roughly the same either with nymph or wet fly and I plumped again for the traditional wets not least because of their more warming, rhythmic casting and faster retrieve. Those little nymphs I had carefully devised got pushed further and further into the 'little-used' corner of the fly box. Perhaps I will come back to them again however, for despite its drawbacks there is something rather unique about slowly searching the unseen depths with a nymph, never quite knowing if you will hit a fish until there is that wonderful thump on the fly. And if you are nymphing in very clear water you might suddenly see that tantalising gold wink of a trout a few feet down as it turns and engulfs the fly and that does make those frozen fingers and toes more bearable in some respect!

I have found 'nymphing' from the bank relatively more successful than in the boat, but only using sparsely dressed traditional patterns or my own variants. Nymph fishing from the boat is much more akin to wet fly though I have rarely tried it for any length of time. I found that because of the slowing of technique particularly in retrieving, the boat has the appearance, real or imagined, of bearing down on my flies and I just cannot seem to keep good contact with them. This is perhaps where those faster sinking lines and sinking braided leaders come into their own taking those nymphs down to their correct depth before the boat drifts over them. Perhaps because of my hardened roots in traditional 'top of the water' loch style I have not made full use of them! Interestingly exact imitations like a big mayfly nymph when the Caithness mayfly appear have not proved as successful as simply using a bushy wet fly like a Ke He or a Bibio. I know this rather goes against the grain of the 'matching the hatch' ideal but it is my personal experience, others may think differently.

The term 'buzzer fishing' is often incorrectly associated today with 'nymph fishing' when in actual fact buzzers are midge pupae not nymphs at all, however as the technique for fishing both imitations is not dissimilar and 'buzzer nymphs' are part of everyday angling terminology I can see how the confusion has arisen. Buzzers can be fished with the floating line on a long leader using teams of three flies which are very slowly retrieved through the water's surface film and the skill is often rated exceptionally successful for wild trout in difficult flat calms and bright sunshine. Again it is not a technique I would first choose on a wild and windy remote loch, however I have been put firmly in my place when faced with adverse conditions of flat calms, by visiting anglers trained in such southern stillwater adeptness, so it is always worth considering. My colleague Geoffrey Bucknall, well-known fly-tier and angling guru, sometimes has occasion to use a weighted nymph on the point of his three-fly cast when stillwater/loch fishing. Something like a weighted Hare's Ear or Pheasant Tail does well and he tells me this ruse makes all the flies on the leader fish somewhat deeper, the extra weight of the nymph working at depth while the traditional wet flies move in the upper layers of water. Sometimes the nymph is taken by a deeper feeding fish sometimes not, but Geoffrey recommends it as a tactic to try if the weather conditions are fairly still and calm.

Finally, for our big lochs, where the trout are attracted more by move-ment of the fly pulsing in the water rather than because it represents a nymph or a winged insect, I have come to the conclusion that exact nymphal representations are not always essential. I frequently take fish feeding exclusively on stonefly nymphs on something like a Kate McLaren or a Pennel, so do try nymphing as an alternative method but do not be surprised if the fish ignore your beautifully constructed accurate imitation but take a big Black Zulu with gay abandon!

Dapping

'Dapping', 'dibbling' or using the 'blow line' to catch trout is a very old boat fishing technique used on Scottish and Irish lochs. It is a skill rather akin to tripping a bushy top dropper of a wet fly cast along the loch surface before lifting off and it is all about presenting a large fluffy artificial fly to a trout by using a strong wind to its best advantage. In olden days rods for dapping were anything between 14–20ft (4.2–6m) long made of cane or similar, and a silk fly line was used on the reel. On to the end of this silk line was attached about 15yds (13.5m) of 'blow line' which was originally made of a light woven silk material. Large natural insects like mayfly or daddy-long-legs were then impaled on a bare hook and this was secured to the blow line with a short length of gut cast. Today slightly shorter telescopic rods in the 15–18ft (4.6–5.5m) range are used, even a light salmon rod of 12ft (3.7m) will do at a pinch; the fly line is a light floater and the blow line is now constructed of specially made dapping 'floss'. This floss is a very light-stranded cotton material akin to the flosses used in fly-tying. There are big artificial dapping flies like a bushy Loch Ordie available and these are used to great effect avoiding the need to painstakingly collect natural insects and also letting the more squeamish angler off the hook, if you will pardon an awful pun.

The art of dapping whether with modern or old equipment has always been quite simple to execute and many large fish are attracted by this method. It is at its most effective when fished from the boat in a strong breeze – I have rarely seen anyone dapping from the bank – and to do it simply draw off the line and about 20ft (6m) of light floss from the reel, with tippet and appropriate dapping fly attached. There is not much perfunctory casting involved, most dappers seem just to extend the rod skyward and let the wind blow the whole shebang out over the water. The artificial should then dip and dance excitingly on the loch surface and with any luck attract a hefty trout. Though I do not often dap myself I have watched this technique done many times on Highland lochs and admittedly it is quite successful in a strong wind. There are one or two drawbacks however, in that trout in their excitement often leap wildly at the fly and miss it, or alternatively they look just about to snatch it with vigour when it is whipped skyward again by the gale and away from the waiting jaws. There is little or no active casting involved in dapping other than perhaps a roll cast in a different direction and it is a branch of angling which, dare I say it, can verge on the uninspiring especially if no trout are taking an interest and you are sitting in a cold force nine waiting for something to happen.

Dapping flies are always heavily dressed and are tied in large traditional patterns with thickly hackled bodies, mainly in sizes 6, 8 and 10. Flies like the Loch Ordie, Red Palmer, Black Palmer, Green Drake, Badger and Daddies are all popular for dapping but if you are unable to lay your hands on these a big lusty dry fly might do the trick, something like a well-hackled French Partridge or even my mayfly variant the 'Junefly'. Nylon should be on the stronger side, about 4–6lb (1.8–2.7kg) breaking strain will do; this is necessary to take the thump (hopefully!) of that big trout. Hooking fish needs anticipation as rather like dry-fly loch fishing you have to wait for the trout to roll over and turn down on the fly before tightening.

At its best with plenty of surface activity from the trout, dapping is a worthwhile exercise making a welcome change of technique if wet fly is failing to do much, indeed it can be tremendously adrenalin stirring if the trout showing are large. Try it on that next windy day and see what transpires.

7

Loch-Style Techniques II

All glory comes from daring to begin.

ANON

Float Tubing

I have only very recently been converted to this more unusual form of transport around Scottish lochs. Basically it allows you the freedom to float around in deeper water without the need to hire a boat for the purpose. Emanating from America (only the Americans could dream up something like this!) the technique involves using a large rubber ring rather like a circular armchair, flippers and a lot of neoprene to keep warm! To get started clad yourself first from top to toe in the neoprene, some very hardy souls use their ordinary rubber chest waders but I found that very cumbersome and rather cold in early season. Neoprene chest waders with a high back and stocking feet are excellent as you must next don a pair of diving flippers making sure to secure the heel strap tightly. Bigger, longer flippers seem very awkward to get around in but they actually propel you quicker in the water, so go for the largest pair you can adequately cope with and complete your ensemble with a flotation device for extra safety. One of those narrow bar get-ups which do not restrict movement but will gas inflate to a full-size life jacket are good. You are going to feel awkward enough at first, never mind wearing a massive lifesaver.

The choice of tube (also known as a bag) is fairly limited still in this country, mine came via a local tackle dealer and an American import supplier, but having found a supplier choose a tube which has a double skin for safety in case of hitting a sharp obstacle and also with an extra raised cushion at your back which I find indispensable to lean on when flipping this way and that in the water. On the skin of the bag there should be plenty of pockets for storing all the accoutrements you would normally take with you in a boat including coffee flask, net, priest, fly boxes and so on. Note when using the tube I do not wear my fishing vest which normally carries all my smaller items of equipment; I have found it gets soaked around the lower half. Instead I put the absolute essentials (fly box, nylon and floatant) in a chest flap of my neoprene waders and wear snippers on a cord round my neck to easily cut any nylon leader. I use a light rod 10ft (3m) rod, but not my most favourite one, as when learning this oddly delightful art, things tend to get stood on or broken rather easily! The tube should be inflated to its fullest capacity otherwise the ride in the water is far too low down for comfort and once everything is assembled put on the flippers, clip the ring seat in position, and step into the centre of the ring making sure the seat is secure between the legs. Simply lift the ring up like a huge skirt and walk gently backwards into the water, though note it is about this time that you start hoping no one you wish to impress is looking as your appearance becomes more and more like a very large and awkward toad! Once the water level is around the waist or thereabouts sit down in the little seat and low and behold you are float tubing!

Float tubing. Fitting the flippers – It is at this moment you hope no one you wish to impress is watching. (*Barbara Syme.*)

Because the first steps in learning to use the float tube are awkward, though not particularly difficult, it is always advisable to have someone with you to assist your progress as getting in and out of the water is a bit of a trachle (Scots word for a struggle!). If he or she is an experienced float tuber so much the better but if not always start your float tubing off gently sloping shores and on a calm day. Spend time getting used to manouvring the tube before fishing: practise getting back on dry land, propelling the tube forward and back and to one side or another by using the flippers, before you even think of lifting the rod. This is very important for actually making the tube go the way you wish is not quite so easy as it appears and the art of working flippers under a hard rubber ring takes a bit of practice. Remember all movement of the ring (which can be quite energetic) has to be done by going backwards so your flippers come up in front of you and you have to lean back and paddle like mad! To begin with you may find as I did that any strong wind makes you spin around like a cork and successful fishing is impossible, but once you can control the tube better this discomfort should cease.

Fishing for wild trout from a float tube is technically very similar to fishing from the boat or bank and typical loch-style tactics can be used. You are pretty low down in the water and a higher raised arm may be necessary to cast and if you enjoy trickling a top dropper on the surface to finish off the retrieve then a longer rod of 10–12ft (3–3.7m) should be used. However, other than raising an arm higher your tactics should roughly be one and the same. I found that roll casting was actually less tiring; the line might not go so far but that is not a problem. Playing a fish, especially a good-sized trout is dramatic because you are in such close proximity to him and to land the trout successfully a small net is essential. Also keep the priest very handy and rest the fish on the front skirt of the tube to dispatch it, not to do so means you can lose the slippery customer very easily.

All in all using a float tube on Scottish lochs is great fun and just as safe if not more so than using a wayward, poorly maintained and often overpriced boat. Get permission to use the tube on the loch however, turning up to bank fish and then producing one of these contraptions may cause a little friction. Otherwise go ahead and try, you may well find you will never want to go back to those leaky boats again!

Ferox Fishing

You may recall in Chapter 4 my mentioning the fact that Frost and Brown, those eminent freshwater biologists and authors of the classic research book *The Trout*, implied that ferox trout were simply very large trout which had grown big feeding off the smaller fish resident in the loch. This may be true but over the years ferox fishing has achieved something of a cult status in Scotland with groups of anglers dedicating themselves solely to their capture.

As ferox almost always lurk at considerable depth in the glacial waters of Scotland the generally accepted technique for catching them is by deep trolling with a live bait. This tactic has been going on since the days of St John and Stoddart in the latter half of the 1800s and has been dramatically recorded by other slightly more recent writers like McDonald Robertson or W. H. Lawrie. John Bailey in the 1980s pursued the ferox with vigour and his book *In Wild Waters* contains a goodly amount of information on trolling for ferox and is recommended reading for those wishing to use this method, though be warned you may curse the day you chose to go trolling for there are lengthy and often freezing cold periods of gross inactivity.

Is it possible therefore to catch a mighty ferox on the fly therefore and save all that lengthy wait? Well, yes, I have done it, but I have only done it once in thirty years of fishing! I offer the following for those wishing to try it however. First of all conditions are everything and not just from the point of view of a dull windy day, believe it or not, conditions of long drought are often good for ferox on the fly. This is not as daft as it sounds for in low water levels Arctic charr can be caught on the fly on the surface instead of hiding away at their usual forty fathoms. It is believed the charr come up to feed on the quite prolific microscopic algae present in more still conditions particularly during a warm May or June. Now if charr come to the surface then logically the ferox may be following along behind his main food source so watch out! I have seen charr in low water suddenly scatter and skitter on the surface like scalded cats in my local Loch Calder, a known ferox loch, and firmly believe a ferox plundering amongst them was the source of their anxious behaviour. Andy Walker of the Freshwater Fisheries Laboratory, Scotland, did studies on ferox, tagging them in Loch Fionn in Sutherland, and found that far from remaining in one small territory the tagged fish would sometimes travel considerable distances up to several miles, up and down the length of the loch, presumably following their source of food.

A number of years ago I read in *Trout and Salmon* an article by an angler stating that he had caught ferox on a large bushy fly which, by using very long lengths of light line, he had allowed to be blown out over the deepwater habitat of this cannibalistic fish. Unfortunately I have no recollection of the chap's name but I did experiment with his ideas with a modicum of success and am much indebted to him for some very exciting fishing. I tried first on Loch Calder and in low water had the alarming experience of a huge bow wave of a fish come torpedoing up toward my very bushy dry fly, a size 8 heavily dressed Soldier Palmer I believe, only to sink back disdainfully into the depths without touching it; but later I tried the same tactic on a loch near Tongue and made dramatic contact.

Any tussle with a ferox, even on hefty trolling tackle, is breathlessly arm-wrenching, make no mistake these fish are furious when caught and oddly enough I later found a rod snapped in two in the same loch on another excursion. I had been fishing along the bank, wading here and there and frankly as the day was somewhat sultry, found little to inspire on the usual wet-fly tactics. Knowing that some very large trout inhabited the loch and remembering the article I had read, I put on one of my hand-tied, fluffy brown dry flies, dabbed on some gink and cast it out as far as possible. There was little movement on the water so any thought of using wind assistance to get the fly out was out of the question. As it was a breeze was not necessary for suddenly a great brown back broke the surface and rolled leisurely over the fly. 'Good God!' I said, but had little time to react further for as the fish turned down it realised it was firmly attached to something it did not fancy and rocketed off across the loch in waspish angst. My rod bent down in the water like a great U-bend and I found it so hard to control the fight I felt dizzy with exertion. I do not believe it showed itself again on the surface at all, it just kept boring away as hard and as deep as it could. Eventually after much reel winding in and letting out, the great beast appeared but a wave of abject panic swept over me as I realised there was little or no space on the bank to beach the fish. The bank was sheer behind where I was wading and any attempt to drag it up and over would undoubtedly result in the loss of the fish. I moved down the bank with this thumping monster still twanging at the line but at least I could feel him tiring slightly. Still no beach, eventually I decided a boulder-strewn shore was my best hope. As it turned out it was a good decision for the fish and a wrong one for me. The big fish's head came up, his serrated white teeth plainly visible and I felt almost frightened about handling him in case he bit me, silly really but his baleful glare and nasty mouth reminded me of a day spent pike fishing in childhood. As I slid the beast into the shallows, his broad dark back was for a moment below my feet and it looked as big as my hand. 'What a catch, what a prize for a dry-fly fisher,' I thought, fear now being replaced by heady elation. The moment of truth arrived for as I tried to beach him his great head came up against the first rock and the fly slipped from his jaws, I can still hear the little chink it made as it fell against the grey stone. Suddenly released it was all the old boy needed and with one mighty lunge he flipped his weighty body back into the loch and sank out of sight. Though I have since caught some great and good three-pounders (1.4 kg) after this experience, nothing has quite matched the fight or the size of that fish which I reckon, even allowing for exaggeration over the intervening years, must have weighed all of 5lb (2.3 kg) and was probably nearer 8lb (3.6 kg), for his proportions I have only matched with salmon.

Apart from their elusive quality and dramatic not to say heart-stopping fighting ability the ferox is still a considerable enigma even in the 1990s. For example how do they see their prey at such depth for there is rarely any light penetration to depths of 40ft (12m) or more? Why do they appear to migrate over a considerable distance of water when they are such solitary territorial fish? Are they a separate subspecies of trout or just big trout? What is it that makes a trout become ferox, do some trout carry this inherent tendency and others not? Why do some ferox become ugly, toothy, eel-like specimens while others of the same weight are beautifully proportioned? Such questions are intriguing for the angler and the biologist alike and I wish fervently that the ferox may be recognised in future as a species to be preserved and conserved. Would it not be the final irony if this cannibalistic, ferocious wild trout, so predatory on its immediate brethren, actually led the way in gaining better legal protection for all of Scotland's wild trout?

Fly-tying for the Lochs

It has often surprised me that somehow the art of fly-tying for trout seems to be recognised as a dexterity out on its own, somehow distanced from the nitty-gritty skills of wet or dry fly, boat or bank fishing. Fly-tying sometimes appears something to be done in the winter dissociated from the water, perhaps at an evening class or with the local Association. Consequently it is almost possible to divorce making an artificial fly from physically catching a wild trout. Indeed, I have met many quite competent anglers who would never dream of tying their own flies claiming that fly-tying seems to them to be too much of a distant science and something requiring superhuman skills in finger manipulation. This is a pity for when it comes down to it fly-tying is a lovely skill, quite simple really once a few rudimentary steps are learned, and remember the final judge and jury of your fly is not your fellow men but a wild swimming fish. I tie flies for trout alone – they often verge on the scruffy and wispy and I would never dream of entering any tying competition with them, but they *do* catch fish. Whilst it is true pottering around with capes, feathers of every hue, threads, flosses and tinsels may not be everyone's cup of tea, it is an exceptionally rewarding part of my fishing. I can still clearly remember the wonderful elation I felt when I caught a wild brown with one of my own hand-tyings rather than a shop-bought fly.

If you are thinking of tying any loch patterns, and I would hope you would be inspired to do so, I would recommend you keep uppermost in your mind the fact you are tying flies first to attract that wild trout's attention, whether he inhabits a wild and desolate hill loch or a soft balmy lowland water. If you consider that for the first four years of their lives trout recognise their prey by the *movement* it makes (Frost and Brown), then logically you want to construct a fly which has a lifelike quality capable of roughly imitating something that the trout have been recently feeding on. I do not believe that an absolutely exact imitation of a particular form of aquatic life is always necessary; an artificial constructed so that it moves attractively in or on the surface of the water will nearly always perform better than one with unrealistic leaden qualities. Once the trout has been stimulated by the action of your artificial fly in the water he will take it either out of curiosity, out of aggression, or simply because it looks vaguely like something he would eat. When the fish's curiosity is aroused the 'take' will usually be a rather cautious pluck and the fish is often lost if your reaction time is slow. However an aggressive take from the trout is a fast, hard pull on the fly and the fish will usually hook himself; something like a Butcher or a Blue Zulu often brings an aggressive response. If the trout has reasoned your artificial to be a food item the takes can vary from very solid to a gentle sip, but always remember the first thing which attracts that trout is actually the artificial's movement in the water and to achieve this important lively quality in a fly, I tie patterns in size 10 or 12 in roughly three different forms.

First, 'palmered' flies (palmered simply means that the hackle extends from the neck of the fly and is wound round the body to near its tail). Without doubt, the movement of the hackles of a palmered loch fly as they pulse through the water or dance on the surface are their most deadly quality. Favourite palmered flies include the Soldier Palmer (also called Red Palmer), Black Zulu, Bibio, Blue Zulu, Brora Ranger, Kate McLaren, Bumbles and so on, and happily as they are usually constructed without wings, these are all relatively easy to tie. When tying up the fly go for a meaty but not overly plump main body; the fly should have an insect-like body but not too bulbous, and then over-wind it with appropriate hackles. Concentrate on getting the hackles well secured around the hook or they can be shredded by the first grab of the trout and pick them out nicely so that they will pulse as they move through the water. Very bushy wet flies often have two or even three hackles wound in but I personally prefer some daylight showing between the fibres rather than using such a density of hackle it ends up little more than a thick ball of fluff. Most palmered flies are general representations of insects but because of the action they make sub-surface in the water, something like the Soldier Palmer could also be taken for a shrimp complete with trailing skittish legs. The big mayfly imitation I tie, already mentioned in the text as the 'Junefly', is a very rough scruffy article quite thickly palmered, but with the propensity to catch some wonderful trout during the mayfly season.

The favoured colours for palmered flies are combinations of black, red and all shades of brown, but blue fibres make an intriguing addition. Geoffrey Bucknall in his book *To Meet the First March Brown* notes that the colour blue is the most easily seen by trout in dusking, fading light conditions. I would also add that since many of our lochs are peat stained and can give the appearance of dark tarns, it would make good sense to try a fly with a touch of blue; Blue Zulus or Camasunary Killers work extremely well on dark lochs accounting for goodly brownies as well as sea trout.

Other flies tied with a bushy neck hackle alone, not palmered but still without wings, include the deadly Ke He tied originally by Kemp and Heddle on Orkney to imitate a small bee. There is rarely a day on any Scottish loch when I do not give this superb fly at least one whirl. It is a multi-purpose imitation of anything from a snail to a shrimp to an insect and with its red splash of a tail, trout will almost always at least rise to it if not consume it with gusto. The other neck-hackled fly I regularly use is the Black Pennel, again terribly effective when the fish are feeding on snail or a hatching insect like midges or black gnats. Though it does not technically represent a nymph I have always found Pennels very effective when insects are just hatching from nymph shuck to flying insect.

I also tie artificials with wings and a neck hackle, the most popular of this design being the Invicta pattern, but others just as effective are the Alder fly,

Expert fly tier Geoffrey Bucknall at work.

Greenwell's Glory, the March Brown and more of that ilk. Tying in wings to any artificial fly makes things a bit more tricky to construct successfully and I favour fairly thin wings so that the shape complements the curve of the fly rather than dwarfing it in over thick feather. Sometimes by missing out the wings altogether a rather good nymph pattern is obtained indeed simply by clipping the wings off an Invicta quite a good 'Hare Lug' can be obtained, only do this however if you can stand ruining a nice Invicta dressing! The flies are usually quite dull in colour; soft browns, muddy yellows, grey and black, though some interesting adaptations can be achieved with these patterns by the adroit use of fluorescent materials to make the otherwise dull body flash attractively sub-surface. In adding any fluorescent material to loch flies however, I would always urge a light touch, overdo it and your fly ends up little more than a bright rainbow trout 'lure'.

I have found most of the winged flies do the business for roughly imitating hatched flying insects like the stonefly, sedge or olive on the loch. In rough waves when the trout are not too fussy all of the aforementioned patterns are quite multi-purpose: Alder flies catch fish feeding on olives, Greenwell's catch fish feeding on stonefly and so on.

Lastly I like to tie other flies with 'wings', though I consider they imitate small darting fish rather than insects of any kind. These include all the Butcher variants with Kingfisher Butcher top of the list and also patterns like the Dunkeld or Silver Invicta. The flash of silver or gold tinsel on the body should be highly visible; try a little bit of pearl Maraflash wound over the gold or silver for extra visibility or add a short strand or two of fluorescent material into the tail tippet. Wings should suggest the upper half of a little fish's body and they are tied in the usual Butcher way, though very early in the season I have experimented with small dark streamer wings which, when the fly is drawn quickly through the water, make for a very realistic fish imitation. Do not forget that touch of red or orange colour to the fly like that in the Butcher design – both these colours seem to stimulate aggression in wild trout.

Finally in composing any variants do remember the old traditional tyings were developed over many years of trial, error and observation and they remain the most successful for Scottish lochs. By all means experiment and vary materials to make your own adaptations of the great traditionals, but try not to overdo it otherwise you end up with a hefty monstrosity which sinks like a stone! Fly-tying is great fun just like any other branch of loch fishing and when tying always think about how this eventual fly is going to move or pulse through the waves. Think of daylight flickering through fibres, think movement, think wispy and scruffy and bear in mind the final judge of your tying is a humble but very cautious wild trout.

8
Weather or Not

The trouble with fish is that they go on holiday the same time as most anglers do.

ANON

As anglers we are all too painfully aware of the scenario . . . We pack the tackle bag, make the sandwiches, set the alarm, race off to the loch at breakneck pace, drink in its early morning beauty, relax, put on a fly, flick out that first exciting turn of line and what happens? The sun comes out, the wind swings icily into the east and the fish, which up until now had been busily chomping insects on the surface, sink silently back into the shadows and with them go much of our over-inflated hopes of a spectacular bag.

Without doubt the vagaries of Scotland's weather dictate the success or failure of an angling day. Even having gone to the extent of judging the right tackle and skills to apply and choosing an appropriately fishy loch the unpredictability of our climate still plays *the* most critical role, either in fulfilling anglers' dreams or dashing most of their hopes. Yet, almost perversely, having to rely on the eccentricities of Scottish weather some-how makes our angling all the more exciting, being tantalisingly unpre-dictable! Watching the television weather forecast does help a little but note that weather forecasts can be notoriously off-beam for most of Scotland (sorry Met office!) and the weatherman who waves his hand over an area from Yorkshire to Caithness saying 'rain over northern parts' treads dangerously in my book. For example a black cloud with pretty little black peardrops emanating from it does *not* implicate rain over all of Scotland; in fact coastal strips and larger areas of low-lying land are often not affected, or the rainfall may be so light it is nothing more than a faint smirl on the windscreen of your car. Happily over the last few years there has been some improvement in forecasting what will happen on our fishing outings. For example, gales may be forecast for part of the week ahead in the farming forecast usually seen on a Sunday lunch time, unfortunately just exactly *when* they are going to arrive remains somewhat of a sticking post! Many outings or holidays are corrupted by anticipating gales or torrential rain which either never arrive or come a day or two later than expected.

Our angling forebears laid great store by the study of our climate and in days past anglers were generally far more in tune with the elements than today when our modern living dictates we closet ourselves away from direct contact with the weather, living in the relative comfort of big cities, travelling in motor cars and spending most of our time in modern centrally heated homes. In the past we were much more physically dependent on the environment and everything had to be done at a slowly evolving pace, corresponding with the cycle of the seasons and their weather patterns; indeed, the climate was the governing influence on all forms of country life including angling. Theories regarding lunar phases and the tides were followed closely and even non-migratory fish like brown trout were thought to follow the moon's appearance. In Revd Daniels' book, *Rural Sports Vol. 1 – Fish*, published in 1801, he recounts many ways he sees the weather influencing fish behaviour. He claimed, not without some justification, that if the moon was full and bright overnight the next day the fish may feed well in the morning, whereas if the moon was not showing the trout would feed well overnight in the dark conditions and then the next day lie out of sight and 'quiet in their holds'. This makes some sense if you think that trout are light sensitive and may not enjoy the glare of white moonlight, however, while not seeking to deliberately disprove this theory, I have actually fished in moonlit conditions and caught a few trout though not many, and I thoroughly enjoyed the romance of angling into the silent night under a brilliant moon, almost as if in a different and slightly eerie world. Lunar influences have continued to intrigue many anglers particularly if you hold the belief that all fish emanate from sea water and therefore are likely to feed well when high and low tides are occurring. To do this, however, they must have retained their sea-going memory and while there are undoubtedly times when brown trout will feed avidly, trying to prove these occurrences coincide with lunar phases and the times of tides is a complex and lengthy business. For my own part it might just be possible to prove or disprove this theory if I were to fish only at high/low tide and then at other mid-tide times to compare successes and failures under these supposed moon influences. Though I would love to be able to do this, the amount of time I would have to be away from my family would make me extremely unpopular all round and I do not think it good PR work to try it, oh the pains of scientific research!

Moon theories apart, there are many other nationally known sayings and superstitions in existence like the oft quoted, 'dark fly for a dark day' and 'bright fly bright day' or 'dark water dark fly, pale water pale fly' which have evolved from local experience and from the observation of weather patterns. Sometimes they work well and sometimes they do not, but they are always worth trying particularly if you are not entirely *au fait* with the loch you are fishing. Lesser-known sayings like 'low-flying swallows mean rising trout' are actually quite helpful for any low-flitting birds along the shoreline, be they swallows, gulls, sand martins etc., will indeed mean they are flying to gather food and therefore the trout are likely to rise to the same insect hatch. 'Big rocks, big fish' is another maxim which I have found moderately successful; I think I first heard it on Orkney. It works on the principle of boulders or skerries which run out into the loch breaking up a uniform surface and providing food and shelter for the trout. Often the bigger fish haunt these bolt-holes and will indeed be found skulking by the big rocks. All in all following any old wive's tales or similar is better than ignoring them especially when in unfamiliar territory, sometimes they prove astoundingly accurate but sometimes they are not, rather like weather prediction itself!

It is interesting to observe that the modern angler's origins will sometimes make a difference to his skills in weather interpretation. If he is city born and bred it usually takes him a little longer to work out what is occurring in the prevailing conditions, after all he does not live and work in them unlike the country-dweller, who is usually more attuned to the run of the seasons. I recall being out with a local gillie not long after moving to the far north from the delights of urban Aberdeen. We were wandering along in pleasant sunshine on a wide expanse of Caithness moor chatting about nothing in particular when suddenly he stopped in his tracks, raised his head appearing to sniff the air and pointed south-west. 'Rain and gales afore noon,' he roundly declared. Looking out across sunlit heather alive with birdsong and the white bog cotton dancing in time to a soft breeze it was very hard to believe him, but sure enough the weather did remarkably change and a good soaking was had by all. There is a twist to that tale however, as when I questioned him later in the local hostelry on his sixth-sense ability for weather prediction, he took a deep draught from his glass, smacked his lips, winked and grinning broadly proclaimed, 'Saw it on the telly last night!'

To assist you through our unpredictable hornet's nest of weather I think it best if I break down the individual components of our systems as basically what goes on above our heads can wet us, blow at us, shine lights on us and alternately heat us up and cool us down. If it does these things to anglers then it also does them to trout and the fish population respond accordingly, not always in the way we would like! If you think of the trout as a wild creature of instinct living entirely on his wits with an in-built fear of the unknown, little wonder he reacts in far more subtle ways than we could possibly imagine. Something we may not even be aware of like a slight drop or rise in temperature, or a change in the wind speed or direction, may make a considerable difference to fish behaviour though we anglers may not have noticed anything different occurring. While placing natural phenomena into sections for convenience, I must point out that everything is very much interlinked, for example, high temperatures can often accompany high light intensity and may also be accompanied by a lack of rain causing water levels to significantly drop. Trout like steady, settled weather and they flourish best enjoying a 'quiet life' when conditions change slowly rather than rapidly; for example, snap frosts in June or snow in August can have a critical effect especially on young immature fish. Even temperatures, plenty of rain, steady wind speed and generally dull, overcast conditions make for the happiest trout. So bearing all that in mind let us look first at what frequently seems to tumble down on our heads . . .

What goes on above our heads will dictate the success or failure of an angling day. Reay lochs, Caithness.

The Rain

Rainfall or the lack of it plays an important role on the wellbeing of the trout and his loch environment. A wet year with plenty of rain means the loch water is well flushed if you will pardon the scientific expression. 'Flushing' of lochs means the time it takes for one body of water to pass through the loch system and be replaced by the same volume of water. When there is a dry year the loch's self-cleansing system may be considerably slowed down with perhaps a build up of algae and/or silt and these conditions are not so beneficial for trout growth. Rainwater is the principal element in bringing in more water to a loch as it adds bulk to feeder streams and springs. Too much rain is rarely a nuisance except perhaps in the case of flooding or sudden spates which rush detritus and silt into the loch down the nursery streams where young trout are much at risk from suffocation. A heavy shower of rain is often welcome by anglers as just after it stops there is usually a flurry of insect hatches and subsequent trout activity. Showers are preferable to constant 'stair rods' of rain which never seem to stop. Although I have caught the odd fish in such torrential rain I find the heaviness of it depressing. Cold water always seems to creep insidiously down my neck and my eyes grow tired of staring at nothing but little holes being drilled into a grey loch, not very inspiring unless you happen to be over some very free-rising fish. I have the theory that trout cannot see the fly so well in such stair-rod rain; the little holes it makes on the surface must surely look rather like a million hefty flies falling on it and though I cannot prove or disprove this theory I can verify I catch less trout in such uncomfortable conditions.

If I look back over ten years of fishing regularly (every week of the season) in the northern Highlands, the pattern emerges that my bags have been better in years of slightly above average rainfall spread evenly over the year, and they have been less good in dry seasons with only short concentrated bursts of rain intermingled with hot dry spells. It is often assumed that the curse of no rain is the plague of salmon anglers with no water in their beloved rivers, however, trout anglers should be just as wary as flows in feeder streams dry up to trickles and important loch-feeding margins of plants, silt and stones are burnt bald by the sunshine. This forces trout to seek out the less favoured feeding grounds of deeper water and can play havoc with any normal free-rising behaviour. Lack of rain can also mean that reservoirs holding trout see much heavier drawing off of water to meet public demand and some smaller waters can fall dangerously low. Scotland as a whole however, does not usually experience the ravaging droughts of English high summers and if you want a rule of thumb covering Scottish rainfall, the driest months are usually May and June with all other months seeing a fair bit of rain, though just how much varies from year to year. That may sound slightly vague but the subject itself is so irritatingly uncertain!

The Wind

Wind strength, speed and direction determine many things in fishing not least the angler's comfort and safety. Winds which merely create pleasant ripples or gentle waves are welcomed by the angler as they provide a breaking of the water surface, disguising most of his intentions, but as wind strength increases so casting becomes more difficult and a point is often reached particularly in exposed areas, when personal safety is more important than the need to fish. More than once in the Highlands, I have either been blown flat on the bank or had to abandon boat fishing for fear of drowning. Most local anglers already know about the sudden viciousness of Scottish gales but there are still those who completely underestimate their effects and their nasty accompanying 'wind-chill' factor. A good bench mark in judging wind force is that if the loch becomes spattered and marked by 'cats' paws' it is usually time to call a halt. These gusty swirls on the water are a sure sign of deterioration in fishing conditions and the quality of catches usually declines when these phenomena appear.

The prevailing winds over Scotland normally come from a westerly 'Gulf Stream' direction with south-west winds usually bringing some rain. Westerlies can be strong though they do sometimes fade to nothing in the evening, a point worth remembering if your day's fishing has been completely disrupted by gales. North-westerlies often bring hail or sleet especially early in the season and can chill you to the bone on a par with normally uncomfortable northerly winds. The most ugly of winds from an angler's point of view is usually the east or north-east wind which deadens most insect hatches and has little in its favour though actually, mid-season, I do catch quite good fish in east winds providing the overhead sky is dull. South-east winds are a major occurrence during the month of May when they are known in the far north as the 'Helm'. This brought our Viking ancestors sailing swiftly over from Norway and is a feature which can continue through June until July when it usually switches back to the west, originally blowing the Viking ships home again! On the subject of the best wind direction for fishing I have no absolute preference, just that it is not going to be so strong and/or so cold that I cannot comfortably fish, and perhaps more importantly, that is not blowing from the same direction as the sunlight. 'When sun and wind align the fishing is far from fine' is a saying I made up and I have found through years of trials and not a few tribulations that it almost always holds good when hunting the wild trout.

As loch trout usually face upwind for maximum oxygen over their gills, in much the same way they lie facing upstream in a river, if the sun shines directly into their eyes they are dazzled and do not see your fly as well as in dull conditions. Waiting until the sun moves away from the prevailing wind direction will pay dividends.

Where lochs lie in very exposed wind-driven areas there may be little chance for vegetation to establish itself on their wave-lashed shores. Thus shores which lie on the lee side of prevailing winds may have slightly more plant growth and therefore larger fish than those with apparently barren banks. Prolonged gales can also force warmer layers of water to pile up at one end of the loch, an unusual occurrence, but one which is quite frequent in exposed areas. I have experienced this effect first-hand while wading along the shore of a small shallow loch near my home. Rounding the bays I suddenly found myself standing in considerably warmer water than that on the lee shore, a distinctly odd feeling, rather like being in a warm bath compared to the other much colder side.

Strong winds over lengthy periods draw up the bottom of a silty loch and make it cloudy and generally unfishable. This silt can take quite some time to settle so it is well worth examining the general clarity of the water. Conversely a lessening of wind speed causes suspended sediments to fall to the loch base; this clearing process has normally begun by late April or May with water clarity at its best through the more calm summer months. However, algae blooms can also be encouraged by still conditions and warmer temperatures, and any water clarity can sometimes be negated by clouds of microscopic plants and animals. Gales mix water and this also oxygenates it so without wind there can be a dangerous lack of oxygen if calm periods are sustained and lengthy. Normally the further north you go the less likely this is to happen, it seems we in the Highlands are rarely without windy weather!

A final point to remember is that warm air also draws up water from the loch in the form of evaporation contributing to water loss if not supplemented by rain so all in all the winds offer a mixed bag of blessings to anglers and fish.

The Temperature

A considerable amount of the wild trout's life cycle is governed by temperature. Even from the day he is conceived in the coldest tiny rivulet, it starts to play a vital role as the speed of development of the eggs depends on a sustained rise in temperature. Alevins develop considerably faster in warmer water than icy cold. As a growing young fish in the tributaries and streams the little fry are dependent on temperatures being kind to them, sudden frosts or boiling heat waves cause high mortalities amongst young trout. Once fully grown the fish constantly react to heat and cold and the internal body temperature of the trout assumes the temperature of the water it lies in. Thus unexpectedly wide fluctuations in temperature can be life threatening as extremes at both ends of the centigrade scale produce considerable torpor in fish and just occasionally death. In mid-winter trout lie torpid and virtually motionless in the icy cold water. They seem to be able to scale down their body systems to a level just enough to sustain life, rather as if in hibernation. In high summer with water becoming almost uncomfortably hot for them after long periods of sunshine, they also give the appearance of torpor, lying doggo on the loch floor in any cooler water they can find. Again this behaviour is the trout's safety mechanism to ensure they do not expend any more energy than necessary, otherwise heat exhaustion coupled with a lack of oxygen can result in death in extreme cases.

Deep lochs in particular show a tendency to stratify into layers of hot surface water and cold deep-lying water during summer, though this in itself does not often affect the trout it may well affect the way anglers have to fish for them. There is a theory that the fish lie deeper in stratified lochs, just about where the two layers of water meet and that fishing your fly at a greater depth than normal could be successful. I have tried this tactical theory with varying degrees of success; it seems to work well on some lochs but not on others, the loch's general fertility and background conditions have also to be taken into account.

Some warming of loch water temperature is essential for encouraging plant and animal growth – all forms of aquatic life need the stimulation of heat to flourish. A gentle rise in temperature as experienced in the spring, encourages insect activity, stirs up the bottom-dwelling invertebrates like shrimps and pulls trout out of their winter lethargy, encouraging them to feed. The speed of digestive processes and energy expenditure in fish is increased as water temperature rises, thus the trout is forced to seek more food to maintain and hopefully increase its body weight. Remember that this natural process of temperature rises stimulating growth in fish is not greatly affected by geographical position. True, the natural rhythm of the seasons may be a smidgen slower in the north but monster trout lurk in the lochs of Shetland as much as they do in the chalk streams of England; it is usually only the angler who complains of the cold, not the fish. Frost in *The Trout* further backed this up in her research on the growth rates of trout on the River Dart, Devonshire, and the River Forss, Caithness. Despite being at opposite ends of the country the growth rates of trout were the same showing other environmental factors like water fertility to be just as crucial.

In general loch temperatures in Scotland show a slow rise and fall over the year, another plus in the country's favour, and the hottest months are usually May and June with a falling-off of warmth in September. July and August are fickle in that sometimes higher temperatures are sustained through these months, and sometimes not, and they are generally more likely to produce humid depressing weather. Thundery weather and storms when temperatures are muggy and oppressively hot are rarely good for trout fishing, the theory being that trout react to atmospheric pressure. I do not know if they actually do or not, all I can tell you from bitter personal experience is that muggy conditions accompanied by clouds of biting midges drive me insane and are not the most conducive for good sport! However when oppressive conditions lift, perhaps after a thunderstorm and/or heavy rain, there is normally a good fishing period following on so such storms have their pros and cons. Any rise in temperature increases evaporation of water and hot spells often have correspondingly low water levels and/or the appearance of disruptive algae blooms.

The Light

Light intensity is the last of the major weather influences and it plays a crucial part as all plant life needs light from the sun to grow. Lochs where there is low light penetration support poor plant growth and associated invertebrate life and they ultimately usually have a less well-fed trout population. Lochs with plenty of sunlight should offer the reverse but other environmental factors such as the composition of the loch base must be taken into consideration. However, if bright light has a beneficial role on loch fertility, it does not necessarily make fishing any easier! Our wild trout are creatures living in semi-darkness for most of the year and they are distinctly sensitive to strong light, actively sheering away from it particularly when the sun and the wind are coming from the same awkward direction. I am convinced that trout facing into both wind *and* bright sun are effectively dazzled and fail to see the fly well perhaps only plucking at it, an irritation anglers usually refer to as 'coming short'. Bright sunshine directly overhead usually puts down wild trout activity but we in the far north do have a distinct advantage here as only in high summer does the sun actually pass directly overhead. During the early and late months of the year, like April and September, we see the sun move through a lower arc and light is often reflected away from the loch surface, bounced off it in fact, so the light conditions for trout fishing are not quite as hopeless as they would seem.

A Word on Global Warming

As we move into the next century the effects of global warming in changing our weather patterns is likely to become more evident. Though it seems that scientific evidence on the effects of holes in the ozone layer and changes in the atmosphere is still not conclusive, it does appear that we are likely to see more volatile swings in our climate in the future with natural disasters like drought, floods or hurricane winds occurring more frequently. Global warming is also linked to the 'chaos' theory which prophesies that as we go forward in time the amount of unpredictable natural disasters in the world is likely to increase. Certainly in Scotland we already endure an unpleasant assortment of mini catastrophes each year from the unpredict-abilities of our climate. Strong winds and floods are a particular curse further north and I have also noticed that the strength of our sunlight seems much more powerful than when I was growing up in the 1950s and 60s. Of course it could also be that my skin is getting thinner with old age (ha!) and I am just more susceptible to the unwanted effects of sunburn, nevertheless I would strongly urge all those who fish over bright sunlit water to put on sunscreen creams, sunglasses and some kind of head gear as cases of heat stroke with severe headache and dehydration are actually quite common in Scotland in May or June. At the other end of the scale, sudden plunging temperatures and numbing 'wind-chill' factors can cause hypothermia even in August and the inappropriately clad can suffer severe consequences if caught out in unexpectedly cold conditions.

The scientists will still probably be arguing over global warming, the chaos theory and all their potential threats until well into the next century but I for one fully intend to be around to hear their pronunciations and will always err on the side of caution when dealing with the effects of our fickle hot and cold weather systems. I would urge you to do likewise!

The Changing Seasons

In Scottish wild trout fishing it is vitally important not only to know of the probable effects of the weather but also to be able to predict the best times of year, month or day to go fishing. Therein lies the rub, however, for unfortunately there are no absolutely pat answers to these questions. Each time you go fishing, conditions are subtly different and can change quite literally from hour to hour!

The best guide I feel I can offer is to look back over past experience and give you a sketch of the likely conditions which you will encounter over the angling year. Though all brown trout fishers must cast a fly between 15 March and 6 October for those are the seasonal limits, it is important to also look at what the winter off-season has been like, particularly in terms of temperatures and rainfall. Most anglers pay the 'dead months' scant attention but actually a harsh winter with ice and snow and a high frequency of subzero temperatures, perhaps continuing until late May, may alter the quality of the start to their next angling season quite dramatically. Hatches of insect life are much more sporadic after cold winters and the richness in plant and/or aquatic life development is slowed down. This often means the trout are lethargic and hard to move and anglers' successes are likely to be much fewer after a severe winter has put nature back on its heels.

Conversely, mild wet winters with little frost mean aquatic life and therefore the trout, are likely to be much more active, even in the earliest days of the season. High winter rainfall also brings loch water levels up to maximum height and trout feed well on this additional shoreline larder, lingering at the edges in perhaps only a foot or so of water. Having now kept many years of seasonal records I note my catches are on the whole better in March and April after preceding mild conditions, but I would temper this by saying that I only go fishing when I know circumstances are exactly right. Local anglers nearly always do better than the visitor in the early months of March and April simply because they can choose exactly when to go whereas the visitor has to take potluck and may well find he fishes for a fortnight without encountering any decent break in the weather whatsoever!

The first two months of the trout season are noted for volatile swings in the weather; during the space of a week it is possible to see snow, gales, hot sun, frost, rain, hail and flat calms and any length of suitably settled fishing weather is likely to be extremely brief. In the early months, days of any warmth with some early spring sunshine, a few clouds and a riffling breeze are usually best and the warmest parts of the day between 11 a.m. and 3 p.m. normally offer the greatest chance of success. I have found an intriguing time 'gap' before the clocks go forward to British summer time often catching a fish at 12 noon when it is actually 1 p.m. and so on. I do not know what it is that occurs around 1 p.m. other than a fluttery hatch of midge or one or two olives, but this time has brought me most of my largest fish with 1.30 p.m. being the exact witching hour throughout all of the trout season and the early half in particular! In some years the ideal early days of the spring idyll can be few and far between up until about May, but it does vary and if you can seek local honest advice on your chosen area first, good early season catches can be had, it is just a question of being there at the right moment!

Once the seasons evolve from spring to early summer, we usually see some more settled spells of weather coming in with some remarkably hot and dry days occurring during the months of late May and June. The length of this early spell of summer sunshine varies, anything from a day to a month has been known, but you can usually bank on some warming sunshine during these two months. Early and late May is often marked in the Highlands by a prevailing south-east wind which frequently blows at gale force. This is an uncomfortably nasty wind as it blows straight out of the morning east sunshine and the two conditions combine to put the trout well down. Indeed, the necessity to fish only on warm, dull days becomes more marked with the sun climbing higher into the sky and there is much more of a need for the angler to follow the rule about avoiding times when the 'sun and wind align'. Water levels in lochs will begin to drop with evaporation and a corresponding drop in rainfall sees the trout move away from the shallows except when drawn there either from a succulent food store or when foraging late in the evening.

By late June there is sometimes a marked change in fishing quality as regards wading, though it does not occur every year, nor in each water. Small immature trout and parr begin to appear in the loch shallows at this time and the larger more cautious trout move away from the thinning water cover of the shoreline. The use of a boat comes more to the fore, if and when this phenomenon begins, but late-evening wading is still highly productive though the air temperature remains critical. I have caught good trout while fishing well into the dusk and dawn but equally I have caught absolutely nothing except pneumonia if the air is too cool. One final word on May and June is that although we frequently see good catches made in the more settled early half of our summer I would not underestimate the strength of the wind at this time of the year; I have been bowled over by gales in both months, just because it looks tamely sunny from the window of your accommodation does not always mean the day will treat you kindly!

One of my favourite fishing times in the Highlands is early July with its usual run of dull grey, mild days bringing insect and fish activity to a spectacular height before the dog days of August set in and the biting midge

Volatile weather conditions! (*Graham Brooks.*)

hatches become too excruciatingly awful. July's increased rainfall is welcome, restoring water levels somewhat and usually bringing renewed feeding enthusiasm in the trout. A wet, warm day in July with a bit of a wind blowing may be pretty awful for the family but it is great for the angler and from my diaries I see most outings in July have produced fish. Evening fishing is good but fishing all day can be very productive as long as there is no bright sunshine to speak about.

The month of August is a bit of a pig by comparison. In my part of the country it is usually deadly midgy and muggy weather, often with a thunderstorm or two and I cannot in all honesty recommend a great deal in this month's favour. Shallow lochs in particular can become almost overheated during this time and if pressed I would suggest dawn excursions on deeper waters are better than nothing at all, but only if you are not able to fish at any other time during the year. The appearance of small fish fry in the shallows will draw some very large trout in close to the edge again but they are irritatingly flighty unless you happen to place your fly directly on line with a trout busily munching its way through baby sticklebacks. August is still technically supposed to be our summer but it is often plagued with a harsh cold snap of gales at the month's end just before we turn to the soft autumn colours of September.

September is a superb month on the lochs with a core week of pure magic usually around the middle of the month when sufficient rainfall has spurred trout to feed in the shallows once more. Unfortunately predicting the exact time of this spectacular week is difficult and if you are a visiting angler you will usually find it has either just occurred before you got there or begins as soon as you go home! Air and water temperatures generally begin to drop now and rainfall increases; the combination of these effects stimulates trout movements bringing them back 'on the take' after the lethargy of August. Sudden storms of hail and sleet bound together with some fantastic rainbows over purple heather moors make September wonderfully scenic as well as good for fishing and if I have a choice of angling times it would be to go out in this month but always suitably clad! Some spectacular trout are caught during the day in September when bigger specimens move close in along the shoreline to feed up for both the rigours of spawning and the coming barrenness of winter. If the trout are heavily coated in protective mucus and ripe with spawn I would urge you to put them back to let them run nature's course. As trout come into spawning dress at different times, there are plenty of others ready to grab your fly and I would concentrate on them. Evening and dawn fishing are not so productive if the air temperature is too cool though look out for that low harvest moon creeping up over the horizon like a giant yellow eye. More than once I have had to blink hard to believe the spectacular beauty of such a baleful moon glinting on our cool September waters.

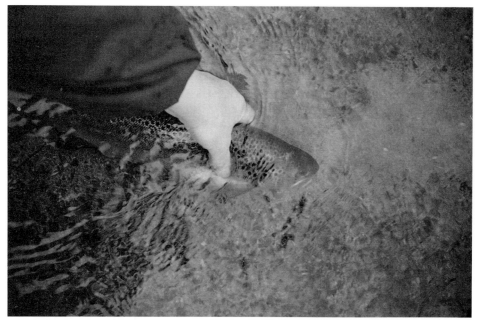

Returning a wild trout in spawning dress.

9
Developing Tactics

What is important is to keep learning, to enjoy challenge, and to tolerate ambiguity. In the end there are no certain answers.

MARINA HORNER

Differences between Rainbow and Brown Trout Techniques

I often act as a guide and tutor to rainbow trout fishers who have become well versed in rainbow tactics but who are unfamiliar with the skills required for the wild brown. These anglers are usually highly proficient and can cast huge lengths of line, fish all number of nymphs and lures, produce endless boxes of brightly coloured flies and switch from a 'slow sink' to a 'fast sink' before you can say Chew Lake, yet somehow put them amongst the vast windy water of a Highland loch and they become somewhat lost, not to say overwhelmed, by it all. As already competent 'trout' fishers they cannot quite adapt their obviously skilled methods to a new fish and a new environment. Thus I feel some information on the topic might assist those afflicted and give a better understanding of the critical differences between brown and rainbow trout fishing.

Let us look at the fundamentals. First the fish themselves are slightly different in the way they behave: the rainbow trout like to obligingly shoal together and swim around their habitat in a group, while brown trout show no such helpful tendencies and skulk largely within a defined territory. It is therefore vital that the angler covers a lot of water to find these territorial browns and I notice that while a number of rainbow *aficionados* loosely understand this concept they still make the mistake of lingering too long over the one spot in the vain hope that a brownie will eventually swim past. Of course he does not and they are often disappointed. Instead, keep casting, move two steps down, wade, cast, retrieve, move two steps down and if there is a boat nearby the angler should always be aiming to wade as fast as it drifts.

Moving apace around the loch is the first essential in pursuing brownies, keeping in touch with the artificial flies is the second. Rainbow anglers often complain of losing brownies because they seem so much faster than the more familiar stockies, yet if they adjusted their technique slightly they would have more joy, though note missing fish can happen to all of us not just the stranger in a foreign land! Frequently rainbow trouters allow themselves the luxury of a wavery line perhaps with the rod tilted skyward rather than parallel to the loch. When our lightning-fast browns take the fly there is just far too much time for them to decide that it is not a 'user-friendly' object and eject it. Keep contact with those flies, think how they are moving through the water pulsing in a lifelike way, and if there is so much as a slight pull, swirl in the water or even a cautious sip at that fly, tighten up to meet it by lifting the rod tip immediately. I understand from one of my southern colleagues that stocked rainbows will often follow the fly quite leisurely and even if they miss it first time they may come back to have another go at it. Wild browns rarely do this, they are just too cautious; if you have even slightly pricked a fish it is rare for him to return to your artificial so always think tension on the line and a quick tightening into any prospective fish.

Regarding tackle, does rainbow trout gear have a place on Scottish lochs? Well most essential rods, reels and lines do, though err on the 'top of the water' floating line concept rather than hefty 'sinkers' as wild browns are not on the whole deepwater hunters and floating or intermediate lines are usually up to the task. Regarding those wonderful concoctions of the rainbow fly box known as 'lures' I would prefer you try the old, traditional brigade first before getting out the Dog Nobblers and the Baby Dolls. I cannot be so purist as to say you should never attempt using them, indeed lures like the Ace of Spades or similar do catch some large brown trout, and of course those lovely brownies will sometimes be so damned fickle they might just take a Cat's Whisker but ignore a Soldier Palmer out of sheer spite! If using lures I would recommend not bigger than a size 10 and not a very heavily dressed one. You might also want to try those 'flies' with beaded heads for, though I personally have never caught anything with them, I have heard of visitors using them with occasional success.

The skill balance on Scottish lochs is not always weighted only toward the 'traditional' man however, for there are times when I have noticed rainbow trouters having much more success than the local wild trout angler. Conditions of heat, bright sun and a flat calm are usually considered of little use on the lochs, in fact I do not fish in such weather unless I have no choice and most locals will pack up and go home in some disgust! Nevertheless I have witnessed my southern friends happily pulling out good baskets of trout while the rest of us wilt in the midday sunshine. When I questioned how they were achieving such good fortune they said the reason was simple, they had to fish in this kind of hot weather all the time at home and consequently had perfected their usual angling technique to cope with both heat and little wind to ripple the surface. When conditions had altered from a nice breezy dull day to bright sun on my local Loch Watten in Caithness, they had simply switched from traditional patterns to the teams of 'buzzer nymphs' they used on their rainbow stillwaters and had attracted around half a dozen or so excellent browns of about the one-pound mark. So straight down the line traditionalists can still learn something from their visiting colleagues and that is as it should be; trying and exchanging new ideas on wild trouting is all part and parcel of the experience and I would not have it any other way.

Watercraft

Good watercraft is fundamental to successful fishing for wild loch trout. In developing 'watercraft' you amalgamate all the knowledge that I have related, skilfully blending your understanding of the environment, the conditions, the behaviour of the fish and the tactics you should be using. Like the good river man who knows his water intimately the expert loch-styler has a deep understanding of all things relating to his angling, fishing in harmony with the natural way of things rather than at odds with them. I think it is fundamentally important to consider and review a loch, its surrounding environment and the day's conditions as a whole *before* starting to fish, rather than rushing headlong down its shores to whip its water to a froth just because there are wild trout in it! And then, once fishing, I will be constantly trying to adapt to all the subtle changes in the conditions and the general 'mood' and atmosphere of the day. Amalgamated skills built from long experience therefore go to make up 'watercraft' and I thought it might be nice to take you on 'A guided tour', as it were, a fishing day together on a Highland loch so that these abilities can be fully illustrated . . .

Let me take you on an imaginary journey to a water neither of us will have fished. Even before we have arrived in the area we will have begged, borrowed or stolen an Ordnance Survey map and poring over it on the evening before our expedition, we can learn much. If the loch has a Gaelic name we may or may not be able to gain an insight into its fish-holding quality (see Appendix II, Translations of Gaelic Loch Names). Nomenclature apart, study the map to see what are the contours of the surrounding land like, are steep leg-aching hills lying in wake or just a gentle stroll across undulating moor or fields? Even if we can simply drive to the edge of a low, level water, the shape of the surrounding landscape is still significant. Where the land reaches its highest point, map contours are tightly packed and these continue down into the loch to show its deepest part. Indeed on very old maps they used to contour the water depth as well as land height thus giving useful navigational charts for fishers as much as everyone else.

The highest side of the loch therefore, is also usually its deepest part and if there is little sign of vegetation and/or shelter there, this area may not sustain many of the larger fish if little food is present and it would probably not be the first place we would try together.

We must look to see if there is a man-made dam on the loch for as we know many of Scotland's lochs provide water as reservoirs for nearby conurbations, large or small. This might lead to soft margins and fluctuating water height and it may also create an extremely deep cold area of water at one end of the loch and a more shallow, pleasantly fishable area at the other. The loch's height above sea-level is very important as the colder air may decrease the winged insect activity and trout may find their main sources of food like shrimp or caddis hugging the bottom. Higher situated lochs also seem to 'warm up' later and can be as much as a month behind the natural rhythm of the seasons. They may also become shrouded in low cloud or mist which makes navigation very difficult and seems to put fish activity down.

Some maps will show boggy areas, some do not, but it is fairly safe to assume that in lower-lying areas of land with an outflowing stream crossing them there could well be some marshy ground best avoided if walking. Counting the number of spawning streams will also give a good idea of the recruitment of young fish to the loch (numerous streams usually mean numerous small fish), and normally it is easier to count the streams on the map rather than at the lochside when many are not immediately obvious. These streams are also important providers of nutrients and minerals usually advantageous to fish growth and any water ingress to the main body of the loch is likely to harbour plant life, invertebrate life and therefore, fish! If we are fishing early in the season it is possible over-wintered non-spawning fish may be present close to these burn mouths and if they have fed well they will make a prize for us to bear home. If however we fish mid-to late season burn mouths may only provide us with young immature fish little more than parr size.

Without further ado let us assemble ready for the off. Let us take in the surroundings which may be anything from grand towering mountains to soft farmland terrain and from peat bog to hidden corrie-like lochs. The lie of the land will tell us much about the likely loch fertility and it is no hardship to observe as it is usually so beautiful anyway. Once we have reached our intended loch destination we should look at the surroundings and shape of the loch. A long, thin, narrow strip of water may mean a trough-like loch with deep icy centre and the fish population may well be hugging the sides for food and shelter. A loch which is indented, studded with an occasional island and lying in a fairly shallow basin may well suit our needs best.

When we choose where to start fishing we should look for anything which runs out into the loch breaking up its uniformity. Underwater features like skerries (partly submerged rocks and boulders), edges of weed beds, reefs, edges of bays and drop-off shelves, promontories, islands and so on are the trout-holding areas. Where shallow water begins to deepen, anything from 2ft to about 10ft (60cm–3m), is probably ideal, but as long as the water has invertebrate fodder and shelter present, is neither too hot nor too cold and is reasonably pure, there could be trout around the feeding areas.

A glance at the amount and variety of bird life is also quite revealing when assessing the loch. Swans and ducks will often up end over weed beds and the trout are also more than likely to be in their vicinity seeking out the invertebrate larder amongst the plants. Swallows, sand martins and other birds suddenly taking off in unison and flitting along the shore show that an insect hatch or two is occurring and trout again are also likely to be on the go. The heron and rarer diving birds like the black-throated diver will gather their main sources of food from small trout and stickleback; trout too enjoy small fish and will be lurking in the vicinity! Note, an over-abundant head of gulls can lead to trout containing worms if a parasite they excrete is eaten by sticklebacks and subsequently eaten by trout. Having said that, I have encountered very few waters apart from a small stank, where this has actually happened; usually the trout population are sufficiently spread out to avoid the scourge of parasites. So even if you cannot see the fish, watch the bird population for a few clues as to their where-abouts.

As we put up our rods to cast that first fly a look along the shoreline will not go amiss. The colour and overall feel of the landscape can be indicative of what lies within the water. Lush greens, soft moorland browns, purpled heather, shrubs, deciduous trees, rolling farmland and so on will often contain good fish populations but this must be qualified by the fact that even the most uninspiringly bleak looking mountain tarn can hold good trout. Lochs with limestone, sandstone or marl present usually have a paler shoreline and lochs with a mixture of white stones (*Clach Geala* in Gaelic, see Appendix II) are almost always fertile with sizeable fish present. Scuffing around in the vegetation of the bank will give an idea of what flying insect population are likely to settle on the loch and bring up fish; in fact if you do this on a leeward shore you will often see a sudden burst of fish activity further out as the insects drift off *en masse* toward any waiting trout. It goes without saying that any long grass, weeds, trees or shrubs will usually produce much more flying insect life than bald, barren shorelines with no cover from the excesses of the elements.

And what of the water itself? Is it dark and stained with peat runoff or is it clear? Note that waters which lie over a dark rock base may appear to be peaty holes and therefore of not much use to the angler when in fact if you take a sample of water from them and hold it against a white background the water is quite clear. Lochs can be anything from gin clear to the colour of sweet sherry with all shades of weak tea in between. In the most general of terms the clearer the water the larger the trout but very clear waters can actually be quite acidified from forestry and/or acid rain. Is the loch cloudy at all? A water which carries a sediment, be it silt or algae may be more difficult to fish than one which is clear. Although trout see well over some distance if water clarity is lessened it usually takes them more time to see the fly. Very murky water also carries with it poor light penetration and subsequently poor plant growth, not so good for the fish. Is the water hot or cold to the touch? Shallows which are warm will indicate lengthy periods of sunshine and trout may be lurking well offshore in the cooler depths. Let us have a glance at the natural feeding on the loch bottom. Puddle about a bit in the shallowest margins, turn over some stones, look for shrimp, nymphs, caddis larvae and/or snail populations. Are there any sticklebacks and their fry present? You already know the presence of shrimp indicates a more fertile loch but if there is any prominent surfeit of a food item in your sample such as stonefly or midge then the trout are likely to fix their feeding patterns on them – remember the 'abundance theory' already explained!

There are various rules of thumb which can help in choosing our artificial flies for the loch – selecting a fly to match the water colour, 'dark water, dark fly, pale water, pale fly' is one. 'Big wave, big fly' and vice versa is another. However, if we are both completely unfamiliar with the water I would recommend a couple of slightly differing traditional black flies first, perhaps you a Black Zulu and myself a Connemara Black to ply on our

The author works down a shoreline fishing across the wind on Loch na Coarach, Sutherland.

floating lines and 4lb (1.8kg) nylon. We will work our way steadily down the shore casting across the wind, with the light fairly dull behind cloud cover at the moment. You raise a fish and I another and things look hopeful. We bag a few and then about noon the wind drops, sending an almighty flutter of sedge skittering around the water's edge. Dark stonefly and olive are mixed in with brown sedge and we change our flies to dry, you a dry Wickham's and myself a dry Invicta.

The sport is fast and great fun when we notice the sun is burning away the cloud cover and conditions are becoming brighter every second. Another tactical change perhaps, with you using an intermediate and myself a floater and we use teams of buzzers left to drift gently in the surface film. By mid-afternoon the cloud cover returns and the wind gets up blowing a hard gale from the south and west and we change quickly back to bigger wet flies and floating lines for another burst of sport. You will have observed that throughout the day there have been 'witching hours' or key times when fish activity will start or finish, usually coinciding with a change in air temperature. These times usually occur around sunrise, 12 noon, 4 p.m. and then again at sunset and will coincide with a 'rise' from the fish which may last five minutes or an hour or more.

When we end our day tired but happy we see we have about six trout to take back but they are of goodly size and we have returned many more. The walk back is happy and our laughter echoes across the moor, for the time being we are content with our fishing world.

10

Tactics from Around the Country

Winning can be defined as the science of being totally prepared.

GEORGE ALLEN

It is well known that the most successful anglers in the sport of loch fishing are the ones who have taken the time and trouble to become highly familiar with their local waters, fishing them in all moods, all weathers and in all seasons, for only then can they say with reasonable accuracy whether one particular tactic will work better than another. However acquiring local knowledge is not always as easy as it seems, especially if you are a visitor with limited time available, so I have sought out some advance expertise from various regions around Scotland which should considerably aid your quest for the wild loch trout.

Comparing localised techniques from around the Scottish mainland turned out to be an interesting exercise, for though most of the anglers questioned used broadly similar traditional loch-style tactics, here and there they had their own subtle local variations, be it a particular fly or a particular way of fishing, and it is these I seek to highlight. So without further ado let us go and 'seek local advice' from anglers well versed in the skills required for their own area . . .

Wild Side of Argyllshire

Scottish Ladies' National champion (1993/4) Jane Wright has fished around the wilds of Argyll for twenty years or so and her usual tactics for the wild brown of these parts are to use the traditional floating or intermediate line (very occasionally a slow sink for added depth) and a team of three flies, sometimes four in a big wave. Her most favoured choice of wet flies includes Kate McLaren variants, Black Zulus, Orange Bibio, McLeod's Olive and a fly called the Joey, which is a black spider tying with red head and red tail (something akin to the Brora Ranger). Sometimes Jane uses a wee double like a double Dunkeld on the point to give the whole leader extra depth, an interesting tactic rather like using a weighted nymph. About 75 per cent of her fishing is done with the wet fly but the dry fly is by no means excluded and Mini Muddlers and Elk Hair Sedges have proved very effective when fish are active on the surface. For more variation Jane will sometimes use a team of buzzers like the Shipman's Suspender or Polywing midge, fishing these slowly in the surface film.

Jane places considerable emphasis on the depth and speed at which these flies are fished for as she says, 'To be effective your flies must be fished where the fish actually are and in a manner which is attractive without being frightening.' Thus Jane will change lines and flies comparatively often to find the correct depth at which the fish are feeding and will occasionally use the tactic of matching the hatch. She ties many flies herself and is a great believer in creating flies which move well in the water with a strong silhouette; she has a particular liking for the McLeod's Olive made with dark grey starling wing, gold butt, green body, gold rib and green hackle. In Argyll generally, Jane recommends the months of May and June for the better wild trout fishing and the Protected waters of Loch Avich and Loch Awe are two of her many favourites.

Caithness Classics

Caithness is of course my main stomping ground for loch fishing but as I have already expounded in considerable detail on personal styles and techniques I felt it would be appropriate to hear from a young local angler who has grown up in an area quite rightly renowned for its wild trout angling. Alan Porteous has fished around the county for approximately fifteen years and during that time has participated in the Scottish Youth National Championships and is the current 1994 Dounreay Club (Senior) Champion. Though still in his twenties his comprehensive understanding of wild trout angling is to be admired and Alan can be found regularly plying a fly on Loch Calder, Loch Watten, the Reay lochs or Loch St Johns. His tactics are very traditional and he uses about 90 per cent wet fly with a 10 per cent adaptation of dry fly, say a dry Greenwell or dry Black Gnat, which he would use in a flat calm. A typical wet three-fly cast used on the floating or intermediate line would consist of the bushy Bibio as top dropper, Greenwell's in the middle and Silver Invicta or Connemara Black on the point. Alan makes most of his own flies and also likes to fish the Olive Bumble and Hopper variants which he ties in all shades of brown, black, yellow and green. He rarely uses a sinking line which coincides with my own thinking for this area, preferring instead to vary the speed of retrieve of a floater or intermediate to achieve the appropriate fishing depth. Alan uses a 10ft (3m) rod from the bank, and a 11ft (3.4m) from the boat, which better assists working the top dropper, and is a great believer in constantly adapting technique to suit the prevailing weather conditions (which in Caithness can change hourly!). He finds his most successful times of year are usually the months of May and September and suggests an evening drift on Watten from about 8 p.m. onwards for some really exciting fishing – hear, hear!

Clydeside Days

Although I lived for over nineteen years in close association with the River Clyde and the Glasgow area I must admit I cannot recall ever visiting the waters of South Lanark and the Upper Clyde. This was most remiss of me for there are some secluded little reservoirs with wild browns in this area and they number amongst them the Daer, Camps and Logan/Dunside waters. All of these fall under the River Clyde Protection Order. Bill Rintoul, who has fished in this region for around eighteen years, tells me his tactics for the local lochs are adapted according to the seasons with mainly wet fly on floating or intermediate line early on, a change to dry fly about mid-season and then he enjoys dapping in September time. Because the lochs in the area are of high altitude there tends to be little surface activity early in the season and teams of nymphs can also be used with good effect. Three-fly casts are the norm for wet fly and nymph fishing and the most successful patterns for the area are usually of dark coloration. Grouse and Claret, Pennel variants, Bibio, Coch Y Bondue and dark palmered flies are very useful normally in size 10 to 16 and note that they are often 'Clyde dressed' which means they are more sparsely tied than the bushier, Highland varieties.

The waters here are clear with a slightly alkaline pH (7.4 in Daer) and natural feeding is of the midge, shrimp and beetle variety with good terrestrials like Red Legs (Bibio fly) and Daddies later in the year. Dapping with artificial Daddy-Long-Legs from the boat offers good sport on the Daer water and Bill particularly enjoys a late evening drift here with a single dry fly, usually using a Roof Winged Sedge or similar. Though he does not use it himself Bill has seen the 'Dundee Cast' used locally in the area and this is an ingenious method of fishing the tippet with three flies but they are tied straight on the nylon line without droppers. Stan Clements, who hails originally from the Clyde valley, still uses this method of tying on flies to the leader today (see Tyings from Tayside) and it is nice to see the old traditions being kept alive around Scotland as a whole.

Fort William and Lochaber

Douglas Kyle of the Rod and Gun Shop in Fort William has fished around this grand mountainous area for twelve years or so and particularly enjoys the trout fishing on Loch Arkaig and Loch Lochy. The lochs in this wild mountainous region tend to be on the big side like the hills above them, and consequently boats may be required to do them proper justice. However, bank fishing is at times very productive and for those prepared to trek there are some good smaller hill lochs off the beaten track particularly to the north and west of Fort William itself.

Douglas advises using the traditional floating or sink-tip line and flies like the Zulu, Bibio and Soldier Palmer (sizes 10–14); indeed most of the darker tyings of flies do well here. Dunkelds can be very effective as an early season 'lure' pattern and note that the higher altitude waters can have a later hatch of natural insects than would normally be expected. The heather moth hatches can be quite prolific in season and any general imitation tied with a bushy brown/grey hackle is effective. Midge, stonefly and olive are the usual natural insects found in this rugged area and locals will tie up large general representation 'Mayflies' which are fished dry to great effect from late June when the surface activity improves. Douglas advises that Loch Arkaig, which has recently applied for the benefits of a Protection Order, also has ferox present amongst its brownies though these are normally only taken on the troll rather than the fly. He states that lochs like Arkaig tend to go off slightly in late July and August before they pick up again in September; however the smaller high hill lochs may be fished right through the year, from perhaps May, depending on the severity of the winter. Excellent trouting can also be had in the Invergarry, Invermoriston, Tomdoun, Glen Moriston and Acharacle areas and Lochaber offers the visitor splendid hills and wild trout in very grand scenery. Highly recommended not only by Douglas but also myself!

Inverness Intrigue

Although this area is one I visit a lot I never seem to get enough time to do its fishing justice and therefore speaking to John Hamilton of the Inverness tackle shop, J. Graham & Co., was of great assistance. John advised me that most local anglers including himself, a trout fisher of some thirty plus years, will use the traditional loch style techniques with a three-fly cast and floating or intermediate line. A number of anglers use the slow sink line, especially early in the season, and typical casts are made up from flies in 10s, 12s and 14s like the Pennel, Zulu, and the Soldier Palmer. The top dropper is usually a good bushy specimen perhaps tied with a badger hackle for good tripping across the waves in typical loch-style fashion. Muddler minnows are also popular in this area and nymphs like the Hare Lug fished on a slow retrieve, are also used with some effect.

The lochs in this area especially the group of lochs to the south of Inverness like Ruthven, Knockie and Bran, can be reasonably fertile with good hatches of olives, midge, sedge and some mayfly is said to be present on Loch Ruthven, also a personal favourite water of John's (and mine!). Depending on the preceding winter John advises the lochs will get going from April on with the best months being April, May, June and September and do not forget to try the lochs to the west of Inverness in the Cannich area like, Beannacharan, Benevean, Monar and Mullardoch where these traditional tactics will work just as well.

Lothian Delights

Drew Jamieson FIFM is a highly respected fishery manager with Lothian Regional Council and has enjoyed some twenty years of trouting on the Lothian reservoirs, regularly visiting the wild trout waters of Gladhouse, Meggat, Talla, Harperigg and Whiteadder. These are quite challenging clearwater reservoirs and Drew believes in matching the hatch as much as possible. He uses traditional floating line and small flies (14s) favouring the Pennel, Blae and Black, Bibio and buzzer patterns, and selects larger patterns only in the biggest of waves. As the trout tend to feed mainly on black chironomids he finds black artificials work best during the months of May and June, generally the most productive times. These flies are particularly effective for fishing at dusk when the sedges may appear in quite some number. About 70 per cent of Drew's fishing is wet fly and 30 per cent split between dry fly and dapping. The most popular venue for dapping is Meggat where good results are achieved by the locally tied dapping flies – the 'Dancing Lesley' (no relation!) and the 'Jinking Jenny' made by Mr Keirnan of Yarrow. Drew particularly enjoys dry-fly fishing on Gladhouse from the boat in the lee of the islands, and placing a dry black gnat (tied as the Irish Duck fly with a flat wing) amongst the edges of the ripple brings him some excellent trout. Though Drew is much of a traditionalist he notes quite some success being achieved on the wild trout reservoirs of Lothian by English visitors using weighted nymphs and shrimp imitations, so there is scope here for some exact matching of the hatch either in nymphal form and/or other invertebrate life if desired.

Note that the reservoirs in the Borders region come under the benefits of the Tweed Protection Order and proper permission is required. Lothian Region publish a helpful booklet detailing the fishings on offer.

Perthshire Parade

Harry Davidson, Scottish Field Secretary of the Salmon and Trout Association, has fished around the Perthsire hills for some forty years or more. His travels within this big county have taken him to all variety of lochs large and small and some of his favourites lie in the Dunkeld, Glen Isla, Blairgowrie and Crieff areas. Throughout Perthshire the best times of the season seem to be May and June with the late nights of June and July particularly productive. Harry confirms his tactics are very much along 'old school', traditional lines using floating line and established patterns like the Soldier Palmer, Pennel or Kate McLaren in sizes 12–14 normally on a three-fly cast. Harry does make some more modern additions to his tackle by using an intermediate braided leader which he says greatly assists in getting the tippet down to the correct depth. Although usually using a floating line from the boat during most of the season, Harry recommends a slow sinking line in March or April and the judicious use of an intermediate as required. Most of his trout fall to teams of wet fly though he will use dry fly in the late evening preferring a traditional dry Wickham's or a Split Wing Greenwell which he ties himself. Harry also makes his own wee doubles which he still uses occasionally on the floating line and these have been begged, borrowed or stolen by friends to find success on diverse lochs the length and breadth of the country from Loch Leven to Loch Watten!

In fly-tying Harry does agree with the concept of matching the hatch and prefers first to simulate the outline of the natural insect and then its colour which he points out quite correctly is usually that of a 'wee black beastie'. Preferred colours in Perthshire flies are therefore black, brown or grey with the odd splash of red as an attractor. A considerable number of the Perthshire lochs come under the auspices of Protection Orders with waters in the Tay, Tummel, Garry, Tyndrum and Loch Earn areas all covered by such Orders, which make it illegal to fish without permission or by a means not prescribed with the permit.

Roving in Ross-shire

Bob Brightman is a fully qualified REFFIS and STANIC instructor working out of Evanton in the beautiful county of Ross-shire. He has around thirty years' experience of trout fishing in the region and particularly enjoys the fine lochs of Wester Ross in the Aultbea and Elphin area. He does most of his wild trout fishing from the boat relishing a drift on Cam or Urigill where some of his best fishing days have been experienced. His tactics are largely wet fly on WF floating line and he uses a tapered nylon leader from a 3, 6 or 8lb (1.4, 2.7, 3.6 kg) tippet rather than the modern braided leader of today.

Occasionally if the trout are lying somewhat deeper he uses a sink-tip floating line, a tactic I recall my father using in the 1960s and 70s, so it is good to see traditional methods being continued. For the Ross-shire wild trout lochs he favours the Bloody Butcher on the tail and the Kate McLaren, Peter Ross, Invicta or Bibio, amongst others, for the droppers fishing these in teams of three, occasionally four, in a big wave. A good local wet fly he recommends is the 'Calbreac' which is tied like a variation of the Black Pennel with badger hackle, black body, yellow or green tail and a silver rib. Bob finds the most productive times for trout fishing in Ross are during the months of May and June, but it is also possible to enjoy excellent fishing at the end of July when bigger natural flies like the crane fly make their appearance. When daddies are on the lochs he uses a locally tied pattern called the 'Dad's Daddy' tied by Tony Martin of Golspie. This has a bushy badger hackle, knotted legs, fluorescent green tail, red body and is ribbed with black tying thread. It is extremely effective as a dry pattern and can be used from May through to September with great effect even when no crane fly are on the water. Bob cites the time he fished on Loch Beannach (Sutherland) and had the 'Dad's Daddy' drooped over the side of the boat while changing a fly. A real daddy flew up to it and tried to mate with it and then a trout came up and took them both – a great testimony to the fly's effectiveness if ever there was one! Other artificial dry flies used on the floating line are heavily dressed dry sedge patterns and Bob finds these especially effective in the evening on a top dropper, though he states that over many years of Ross fishing he has found most of his good trout tend to come to that sleekly dressed Bloody Butcher on the tail.

High Sutherland Hill Lochs

Billy Faulkner, a well-known local angler from the village of Scourie, has fished around this wild district of Sutherland for over forty years. During that time he has remained faithful to traditional top of the water floating line tactics with roughly 80 per cent of his trout fishing success achieved with the wet fly. Most successful patterns for the hill lochs include the Soldier Palmer, Black Pennel, Invicta and Connemara Black, and Billy uses these on a three-fly cast except when the loch is weeded when he will only use one or two flies. Visiting anglers do use intermediate or sinking lines in the area but, as the wild trout are mainly found in the shallows rather than the infertile deeps, Billy advises using the floating line first. Most of his local success has come from using traditional 'wets'; however, there is scope for the occasional switch to dry fly or dapping especially when the daddy-long-legs appear later in the season. Dry flies are very effective when worked on the top dropper of an otherwise wet-fly cast and a dry Soldier Palmer or

Black Gnat does exceptionally well. Muddlers fished on the top dropper can also be effective when sedge appear on the lochs. The natural feeding around here varies from loch to loch but there are outcrops of limestone running all along and across most of Sutherland from Durness to Forsinard, and surprisingly fertile waters are commonplace around Scourie and the Reay Forest area. Shrimp, caddis, beetle, snail, stonefly, midge and *bibio* (heather fly) are all found in the region though the proportion of each life form depends on the acidity of the water. Billy recommends being prepared to alter your fishing tactics according to the weather conditions; for example, he has occasionally found great success with an Ace of Spades lure dressing when fish have steadfastly refused the traditionals for the area. Usually the most productive months of the year are mid-May to the end of June with another burst again in September. Be prepared for long walks, wild scenery and the odd very large fish amongst the smaller ones.

It should be noted that at the beginning of 1995, Scourie and the Reay Forest area, parts of Rhiconich and down toward the Kylestrome district had a Protection Order granted, making it illegal to fish in the area without proper permission. This Order covers some 600 plus lochs in the district but visiting anglers should note that the cost of a permit is minuscule when considered against the amount of quality fishing now available.

Tyings from Tayside

Stan Clements has been fishing for wild trout for over forty years around Scotland, and within Tayside he concentrates his efforts on the Lintrathen, Crombie and Monikie waters. He is a member of the Kincordie Angling Club and a very gifted angler not least in the fly-tying department where he constructs his own flies by hand without a vice, a rare skill to find these days. Stan is what I would term a 'thinking', intuitive angler; indeed, when I asked him what his usual tactics for the wild brown were he immediately said 'think natural'. His whole technique is based on tradition yet it is highly innovative; he uses a 10ft (3m) rod and floating line, but on to that line he attaches a hollow braid (not a braided leader!) of around 3–4ft (90–120cm) and then a nylon tippet of 3lb BS (1.4kg). The hollow braid is actually some old Milbro material no longer made but Stan thinks it may be possible to obtain something like it from modern backing lines. This braid allows a very gentle sinking tip action to the line and takes the fly down to a depth of roughly three feet. Stan will then put two to three flies on the tippet, using the ingenious 'Dundee Cast' which ties in the flies straight onto the nylon thereby avoiding ugly dropper knots (see also 'Clydeside Days'). His usual first choice for wet flies would be Spider, Nymph, Palmer or Sedge tyings in the colours grey, black or turkey brown. He states that approximately 60 per cent of his fishing is with traditional wet fly but a goodly 40 per cent is dry fly with dry Greenwells or Pencil Sedges successful right on the surface. His wet-fly technique leans much more to nymph fishing than most traditional loch-stylers and he is fond of tying up rough nymphs, which he calls his 'Rough and Readys' and makes particular use of both traditional and modern materials for a lifelike effect. At the head of his nymph patterns he usually ties in some of the fluffy 'flue' part of the feather (the part we usually discard) and this he says gives a nice movement to the fly. He will also tie up nymphs with those little gold-beaded heads and he finds considerable success from the 'sink and draw' effect these have when they are moved through the water. He also thinks that the little gold bead adds that extra weight to the head which, when retrieved, makes it swim in a way very akin to a small stickleback or perch fry.

Stan is a great believer in matching the hatch and will spoon a fish to see if he can tie accordingly. If the situation calls for a dry fly Stan likes to tie his own sedges at the water's edge specialising in imitations with clear raffine wings which he will tie in roof-shaped or upright. He has an intriguing theory that by making a new fly either as a broad representation or a natural insect he is creating fresh life and fresh movement in the water with his new materials giving a more lifelike quality than those old well-worn flies with their feathers somewhat lacking in sparkle. This is an opposing theory to the successful 'well-chewed' Invicta I have in my own box but since trout do recognise their prey by the movement it makes in the water, new feathers may well do the trick. It works for Stan anyway.

Though Stan is very much a purist in the strictest sense of the word he retains a delightful sense of humour about fishing and we laughed together at his story of a competition he had entered on Loch Leven when he raised a beautiful trout to his carefully hand-tied Black Palmer only for his boat partner to catch it on a huge Black Lure – you cannot win them all!

For Tayside Stan recommends the months of May, June and July but he also likes the challenging difficulties of August when he will tie tiny Caenis to imitate the naturals present then. If you meet Stan you will know him for he will tie flies without a vice conjuring up realistic imitations from the palm of his hand; watch and learn for such talented anglers are thinner on the ground these days.

A Turn Around the Trossachs

Matt Walker is a very 'weel kent' figure in fishing circles having been past President of the Scottish Anglers' National Association for a number of years as well as being an exceptionally knowledgable angler with experience of trout waters all around Britain. For the last ten years or so he has concentrated his angling around the Trossachs and Stirlingshire area frequenting the lochs of Ard, Venachar, Katrine, Arklet and Glen Finglas as well as sorties to Loch Carron. Matt's tactics for this lovely area are highly traditional with about 90 per cent of his fishing being done on the wet fly using a team of four flies with floating or intermediate line, fishing from the drifting boat rather than the bank. Matt will vary his fly selection according to the choice of loch and the prevailing conditions but he recommends any patterns like the Professor, Zulu, Kate McLaren and Bibio as a good first choice. For the top dropper of his cast Matt ties his own fly, the 'Gartmore Palmer', which, with a predominant yellow tinge, makes a good general olive or sedge representation. The fly is tied with primrose seal's fur body, primrose silk, golden pheasant topping tail, gold oval rib and hackles of red game and olive palmered together. It is not unlike the Golden Olive Bumble and many anglers have found great success with it on the Trossachs lochs.

Matt advises that there is not normally a profuse daytime hatch of natural insects on the waters here so that general representations of fly life are usually used rather than exact matching of the hatch. Matt fishes Loch Ard right from 15 March and he recommends this as a fine early loch with the Peter Ross fly doing very well. Loch Venachar provides good fishing during April, May and September and Loch Katrine, Matt's favourite water, fishes well in May, June and September. Natural hatches occurring on the slightly acidic Trossachs lochs are usually midge and olive but there are terrestrials like the daddy and heather fly also present in season. Out on Loch Carron Matt favours smaller flies like the Shipman's or a small Black Gnat to cope with the profuse buzzer hatches experienced there.

11

Modern Influences on Scotland's Trout

Survival is triumph enough.

HARRY CREWS

T here are a number of important external influences which will affect
your trout loch fishing in Scotland. I would refer to these aspects as
legal, environmental and managerial, so let us look at the law first . . .

The Law Relating to Wild Trout/Loch Fishing

There are various legal controls on the welfare of the wild brown trout in
Scotland. Unfortunately they are repeatedly misinterpreted, frequently misunderstood and often, either innocently or deliberately, ignored. I would like
now to spell out the hard facts of the law governing wild loch trout as, like it or
not, the pressures on trout stocks are of growing concern and it is important
that all potential anglers be aware of the current legal situation.

Stanley Scott Robinson QC compiled a comprehensive guide to the
legalities of game and fishing in Scotland entitled *The Law of Game, Salmon
and Freshwater Fishing in Scotland* (Butterworth 1990) and it is worthwhile
repeating part of his analysis of the legal aspects concerning brown trout
fishing in lochs as opposed to river or stream fishing.

'1. No one has any right to trespass upon the lands of another for the
purpose of fishing.

2. No one, even if he is lawfully on the bank of a river or loch under right
of access, has the right to fish in the river or loch.

3. Members of the public, having neither title nor right, cannot establish a
right of fishing by any usage of fishing for however long a period, as against
a proprietor having title over which the stream flows.'

This basically means that the legal right to fish for trout in lochs rests
solely with the proprietor(s) of the land surrounding the loch and only he

can grant permission to others to let them fish, usually by means of a permit. Thus when you are told, 'all trout fishing is free' or 'you can fish there for nothing, it's a public right', such advice is usually nonsense. The only place where trout fishing is actually 'free' is in a tidal water (a loch which has some influence from a sea tide) and though there are a few inland waters which have such conditions, most tidal legalities apply to river estuary fishing and not freshwater lochs.

As the aforementioned laws covering access to fishing on private land have been enshrined in the Scottish civil law of Trespass they are often ignored as the only true way a landowner may stop you fishing in a freshwater loch is to obtain an Interim Interdict against you, which means should you return to fish again on his land you are then committing an offence. This type of legislation is very slow and costly and frankly most landowners will not bother unless you are a persistent offender. However, recent changes in the Criminal Justice Act give landowners much more power in removing unwarranted visitors from their land and it could be that bus party groups turning up to fish illegally may find themselves getting the same treatment as the hunt saboteur or the rave party organiser. I personally feel that providing the changes in the Law of Trespass are not abused by the landowner (the right to roam freely, but responsibly, in Scotland has always been enjoyed by the outdoor lover) then the additional power to stop illegal trespass to fish without permission may prove of benefit. Time only will tell on that one and further developments are awaited with interest.

The law is also very clear on illegal methods of fishing for trout stating that no person may fish for trout in any inland water except by rod and line and that the use of a rod which is not hand-held is illegal. Thus coarse fishing methods when the rod (usually a spinning rod, bubble float and bait) is propped up on a rest is regarded as a 'set line' or 'fixed engine' in Scotland and is a fineable offence. This type of statute is having to be enforced more and more in the Highlands when a number of anglers will arrive on the loch shore with six or eight rods each and proceed to string them out along the bank taking every unfortunate fish they encounter. In Caithness recently a visiting angler was fined over £200 and had his fishing gear confiscated, when he used a set line on our 'fly only' Loch Watten. If you see any such activity on your local waters, get a witness and report the matter to the police. It is probably wiser for personal safety not to confront the 'anglers' yourself, a sad indictment of some of the more unwelcome influences on our lovely sport.

There is a statutory six-month close season for brown trout and no fishing for browns may be undertaken between 7 October and 14 March every year. Rainbow-trout fisheries, however, do open for much longer periods of time and do not have the same restrictions in close seasons, though note where there are a mix of rainbows and browns in a loch, the brown trout, if caught out of season, must be returned.

Protection Orders

You will have noticed when looking at the local tactical advice culled from specific regions of Scotland I mention many waters as being 'protected'. In any water forming part of a protected catchment area, even if it is a remote loch apparently not connected to the main watershed, any fishing without permission becomes a statutory offence with the possibility of a hefty fine. This may sound slightly discouraging to the potential angler, but such Orders if properly constituted and properly supervised, do offer the chance of much better regulated fishings and the poaching activity of set lines or similar is normally well reduced on protected waters. Waters covered by Protection Orders in Scotland are growing and they now include Loch Awe area; River Tay catchment area; River Don area; the Tummel and Garry watershed; the Tweed catchment; West Strathclyde and the River Clyde catchment; the Scourie, Rhiconich and Kylestrome area of Sutherland and there is also an application in for the Loch Arkaig area of Lochaber.

Protection Orders are issued through the Scottish Secretary of State's Office and do not directly protect the fish resident in the waters concerned, rather they protect the riparian owners' fishing rights on their stretch of water and once granted, it is up to the owner to take appropriate steps to conserve the fish population. For an Order to be granted at all there must be an increase in public access to the waters, access being relative to the likely demand for angling and the Order can only cover a pre-defined area. The implementation of such Orders is often a long-drawn-out process, sometimes involving years of protracted negotiations, and in general the Scottish experience has proved that both anglers and riparian owners find the Orders unnecessarily complicated and often misunderstood. It is perhaps indicative that since their inception in 1976 only eight POs have actually come to fruition.

Usually the Order is granted without a time limit and sadly it makes no allowances for lochs or rivers changing hands with there being no legal method of bringing an unprincipled landowner into line with other bona fide fishing operators who come under the POs auspices. There is no redress, for example, against an owner who suddenly decides to stop public access to his 'stretch' or alternatively doubles the cost of a permit to the public. The only way the rogue riparian owner may be brought to book is by the Scottish Office rescinding the whole of the Protection Order thus completely defeating its original purpose! This effectively means that a PO can be exploited for commercial gain by the unscrupulous who can double fishing pressure without putting anything back into the management of the loch, for example by contributing toward any necessary restocking programmes.

Properly constituted Protection Orders where each riparian owner contributes equally to the common good, working to a pre-established management programme, do work quite well in curtailing illegal methods of fishing and may indeed bring about a long-term improvement in fish management and conservation. I cannot help but feel however, that if the Hunter Committee's recommendations of the 1960s making all brown trout a recognised protected species no matter their location had been accepted then, none of these rather clumsy Orders would be necessary. As it is we have inherited a piece of law protecting landlords' fishing rights rather than conserving a fish at the centre of our angling heritage and paradoxically, prime wild trout areas without Protection Orders are being placed under increasing threat from displaced illegal fishers looking for new hunting grounds. In the long term I fervently hope that all of Scotland's wild brown trout are covered by a proper means of protection and conservation – not to consider a policy like this now may well mean a future over exploitation of our cherished fish.

The Changing Environment of the Wild Loch Brown

When Reverend W. B. Daniel described the habitat of wild trout in 1801 as 'fishes residing in an element little subject to alteration, theirs is a uniform existence' (*Rural Sports*, vol. 2, 'Fish'), he could not possibly have foreseen the dramatic changes modern industrial society could bring about. At first it would seem that how man uses his land would not really affect water-dwelling trout, but unfortunately everything we do to our environment will almost always influence the resident fish population whether intentional or not. Our actions directly control the destiny of wild trout and it is no longer possible to say that they live undisturbed in isolation, except perhaps in the very remote areas of northern Scotland, for today there are a myriad of human and environmental issues likely to affect them. These changes to the environment may well cause a decline in the quality of trout loch fishing though I must add that proving any widespread decline of brown trout stocks in Scotland is a difficult if not impossible task. There is such a complex variety of lochs within the country all containing different numbers and sizes of trout, and even if records have been kept of fishings they only give isolated pictures of the ups and downs of one particular water rather than a nationwide statistical picture. If you put together every catch record book in Scotland, however diligently kept, you would still find enormous gaps in knowledge with thousands of 'unknown quantities' appearing amidst the already charted waters. These unknown quantities vary considerably in character; it may be certain lochs have never been monitored or that catch returns were started by one riparian owner only to be forgotten by another; or it could be that records were constantly interrupted by world events – in the Highlands, for example, many catch returns suddenly cease during or after World War II.

Such lack of continuous knowledge can lead to the appearance of a decline, real or imagined, in the quality of trout fishing in Scotland. As anglers we are all guilty of saying, 'Oh the fishing is not like it used to be', but actually proving this to be the actual case is something else! If indeed there has been any deterioration in the quality of wild trout fishing it will normally have happened over a considerable length of time, centuries in fact.

To illustrate the possible effects of environmental change on wild trout let us look at what may have occurred in an imaginary, but nevertheless typical, large Scottish freshwater loch over the last 100 years or so, for we will see that according to the whims of land use, water and trout fishing quality may have fluctuated quite dramatically over such a period of time.

A Typical Trout Water

The loch contains a reasonable population of wild brown trout which have been added to at various times in the past. Before and after World War I efforts are made by a riparian owner to stock the loch bringing in thousands of small trout fry and these do well amongst the indigenous population. However the restocking policy falls into decline after World War II and by the late 1960s the land and its fishing rights change hands and restocking ceases altogether.

The pH of this theoretical loch is neutral to slightly acid and it is situated in an area of hills, mixed agriculture and moorland fed from rainwater, feeder burns and springs. Original land uses in the area would mainly be agricultural and the farmers may have used varying amounts of different fertilisers on their crops over lengthy periods. These plant nutrients are then washed down into the loch through its feeder burn system; usually the chemicals are dispersed with gales though they may raise the loch fertility slightly. Occasionally in still weather they cause an algae bloom which may be toxic to nearby livestock and to the fish depending on the length of time the bloom affects the water. Raising the loch fertility may not actually be overly harmful to the fish, in fact it may encourage trout growth by adding additional nutrients into the water system. However, angling quality may deteriorate when green scum algae discolours the water and the trout rarely rise and are unlikely to see the artificial fly. But, providing the balance is not tipped into an irreversible eutrophication, some additional fertilisation to an acidic loch does not do it irreparable harm.

Periodically we see one of the feeder burns of our loch flooding nearby fields and a land-owner decides there is a need to secure proper drainage. The stream is deepened and thick silt is washed back into the main loch; this is dispersed but the young trout fry population of the burn are completely wiped out for a year or more. Any natural or man-made disaster like a spate will have a considerable knock-on effect on juvenile fish and anglers may find four years after a massive spate in the spawning area that the numbers of mature fish around the one-pound mark are considerably down on previous years' figures.

Commercial forestry looks a good proposition on some now redundant stretches of moor no longer yielding any grouse to the local estate. Today there are more strict guidelines as to the planting of trees near watercourses but if the afforestation has gone ahead prior to the 1990s the monoculture of Christmas trees may well have been planted in straight ditches reaching right down to the water's edge. In heavy rain the ditches bring flash floods which are disgorged rapidly into both the loch itself and its tiny spawning tributaries, which become alternately scoured out or silted up. Any trout eggs in such silt-laden spates are suffocated and the end result is that the quality of natural recruitment to the loch wavers much more dramatically than prior to tree planting. Flooded forestry ditches replace the original spongy mosses of the moor which previously had dispersed rainwater slowly and naturally over the area, and the forestry plantation scavenges the effects of modern-day pollutants such as acid rain. This enhances the land acidity where the trees have been planted on base, poor (acidic) soils and additional acidic compounds find their way into the loch bringing the pH into an acid state. Less obvious accumulated effects on the trout's environment like the long-term impact of forestry and/or acid rain are largely invisible yet they are insidious and the water quality of lochs can be irreversibly changed depending on the nature of the rock strata the lochs lies on – lime-based soils negate acidic runoff, acid rock and soil enhance it.

Years roll on and a new landowner arrives on the loch taking over riparian fishing rights on a farm fronting the water. He decides a commercial fishery may be a good money-making proposition and by putting ten boats out for hire on the loch, thereby doubles fishing pressure overnight. A different landowner somewhat balances this however, by rescinding all public access to his stretch of loch because of the nuisance factor of anglers crossing over agricultural crops and their dogs annoying his livestock. Another riparian owner finds he can supplement his income considerably from running a caravan park on his part of the loch shoreline. This proves a popular venue for anglers and as the landowner values their contributions to his farming income he turns a blind eye to some unscrupulous fishing methods they are employing. The fish population in the immediate vicinity of the caravan site drops quite dramatically as rows of set lines are strung along the bank and ground baiting is used. Any of the actions of land-owners in allowing, or not allowing, fishing from their loch banks will play a critical part in the long-term angling pressure.

Further up the loch at its deepest part, a rainbow trout fish farm is granted permission to operate and its discharges give cause for some concern amongst the community. When a storm breaks open a rearing tank thousands of fingerling fish escape to compete for the food of the indigenous population. These escapees, if sterile, will not harm the original generic strain of brown trout in the loch; however, the nature of the fishing can be considerably altered when the escapees prove much more aggressive in their feeding habits than the resident brownies and for a time the wild brown trout loch appears little more than a put and take rainbow fishery ...

*   *   *

I could go on but it becomes obvious even from this 'fact and fiction' scenario that most of the pressures which are placed upon our wild trout lochs today are man-made, the results bring mixed fortune and in the long term the effects of these stresses are variable and accumulative. Sometimes the good balances out the bad, sometimes it does not. We can see clearly that according to the riparian owner's decisions as to how he uses his land over several generations, often hundreds of years, a pattern of swings and roundabouts will occur in the brown trout's habitat. Generally one environmental 'incident' in itself is not enough to kill off a trout population unless it is an extremely toxic discharge into a loch; instead, the more usual run of things is a lack of care here, a loss of a spawning redd here, overfishing perhaps and/or a subtle alteration in water chemistry over very lengthy periods of time.

Therefore, if you ask me whether I too hold the fishing belief that 'things ain't what they used to be' I cannot in all honesty say yes or no, any deterioration in fishing quality happens over hundreds of years if it happens at all, and Scotland has so many lochs with so many differing environmental characteristics. What I will say that in certain wild trout fishing areas the picture needs some considerable improvement, for there are a number of regions where it is either a neglected or an over-exploited resource, but equally I do believe that we have within our grasp as a nation of trout enthusiasts, the capability to ensure the wild trout's safe survival for future generations. Other than in matters of obvious gross pollution when there is legal redress available through the local River Purification Board and/or the local Environmental Health department, I believe what is needed is a more determined and united effort to raise public awareness in caring for the wild brown trout and his natural habitat. This is *not* an impossible task. We see organisations like the RSPB doing a wonderful job publicising the cause for rare birds, why do we not do it with wild brown trout, or are fish not so precious to the angler as birds are to the ornithologist? To me Scotland's wealth of wild trout fishing is inestimable and there are a number of bodies like the Scottish Anglers' National Association, the Scottish branch of the Institute of Fisheries Management*, the Salmon and Trout Association and other smaller local angling associations and clubs far too numerous to mention, who are all working toward a sensible approach in conserving and developing our wild trout fishings in ways appropriate to the sustainability of the resource. All anglers who value their fishings can do their bit both by supporting those organisations, which actively work and lobby on the anglers' behalf, and by acting as individual watchdogs for the environment they cherish, reporting any threats to its future wellbeing to the appropriate body. Sitting back and doing nothing while the damage is being slowly done achieves little, if your wild trout loch is being threatened make a noise about it!

Management of a Wild Trout Loch

When in 1991 I investigated an alleged decline in the quality of wild trout fishing in Caithness and Sutherland publishing the findings as a report, I found that around 60 per cent of those with angling interests in the area thought the angling had deteriorated. Forty per cent thought it had stayed roughly the same in quality and 0 per cent thought it had improved. When questioned further why they thought the angling had declined the majority of anglers mentioned the lack of proper management for the wild brown trout in freshwater lochs. But just what is 'proper management', for it seems to me easy to place the blame squarely at the feet of a riparian owner when the management issue is actually quite complex and involves a great many different areas of land and water interest, landowners, anglers and other water-users alike.

Good management stems from awareness of the need for holistic care of the wild brown, and this means much more than selling a permit and/or putting a boat on the loch. A good manager has to know what is occurring in his trout's surrounding environment, what is occurring in the water quality and how fish numbers are altering. Monitoring of fish stocks via catch returns, providing they are diligently filled in by anglers, will give some indication of the present condition of the wild trout stock. For example, a year's returns showing numerous small fish being caught may mean average fish size is decreasing, perhaps through anglers taking too many large fish out. Equally a year when fewer, but larger, fish are taken may mean that the natural recruitment from the spawning areas has decreased and the quality of existing spawning redds may have to be improved. A sudden slump in total fish catches, given that the number of

Restocking may have to be considered if the angling pressure is great. Martin Moore of Inverness Fish Farms at work.

angling visits per annum remains fairly steady, may indicate a need to investigate further perhaps for an environmental pollution incident. Over a number of years of studying catch returns the manager will obtain a reasonable guide as to whether the averaging fish size is increasing or decreasing and whether the numbers of fish caught are lessening.

Restocking may have to be considered if the angling pressure is such that the fishery is obviously declining but I personally believe that all natural methods of maintaining and improving the existing natural spawning should be tried first, and only if this fails should a commercial restocking be considered. If the loch does need additions to its natural stock it would appear more sensible to stock from the fry stage as these trout will then have time to adapt and toughen up after a couple of winters to become almost unrecognisable from the wild indigenous species. Commercially reared brown trout which are added in when they are at a pound or so in weight may make a better catch in terms of size but they have lived most of their life in a tank and fight poorly compared with the natural 'grown on' stock. I understand it is now possible to restock from an outside hatchery who will use your brood stock from your own water – this would be a considerable enhancement to the genetic integrity of the wild trout, rather than buying in 'unknown' fish.

Perhaps the strangest thing about riparian ownership in Scotland is that although any person who owns land fronting a loch automatically has rights to fish in it and issue angling permits, not all riparian owners take a great deal of concern about their wild trout lochs, indeed many show no interest in them whatsoever. Many leave the water and its surrounding environment completely alone and hand over the administration of local fishings to an association or a lessee. Voluntary organisations frequently do a good and difficult job in acting as caretakers for the wild brown, but one cannot help but wonder why there is not a more concerted unified attempt to conserve the brownie as a species. I believe education both in better wild trout fishery management and in raising general public awareness, is the key to the future wellbeing of our native fish and I urge all who love this wonderful creature to support any initiative like the Scottish IFM's in promoting a better understanding in the care of the wild brown trout.

I leave you with one final thought on wild trout management. I remember busily preparing a selection of slides for a lecture on wild trout conservation and management I was to give last year. My two young sons wandered in and sat down, two little tousled heads in front of the projection screen. I ran through the lecture not really aware they were listening for they sat comparatively silent and for once did not interrupt. 'That was very interesting,' said the oldest when I finished with customary flourish. 'Why are you doing it?' Children ask the most shrewd questions at times and I was momentarily taken aback by his disarming bluntness. 'I'm doing it so you two will hopefully have something to fish for when you are my age!' I blustered, but they were unimpressed. 'Oh go along,' I said and began switching through the slides once more. 'Fish!' shouted my two-year-old as a picture of two spawning trout about to procreate this wonderful species of ours came up on screen again. 'Well I suppose I am doing it because *I care* about their future,' I said softly, 'I care about these fish.'

* In 1995 the Scottish Institute of Fisheries Management drew together representatives from all public sectors, from conservation bodies to riparian owners and from local councils to angling organisations. They met with the specific aim of thrashing out a future policy for the care of the wild brown trout while considerably raising public awareness of the cause for better conservation of our non-migratory fish.

12

Classic Loch Trout Fishing

Knowledge of what is possible is the beginning of happiness
GEORGE SANTAYANA

What makes really classic trout loch fishing in Scotland? Is it the excitement of the free-rising fish, or the anticipated drama of that big one finally seizing your fly? Is it that you can be ten minutes from the road, yet feel a million miles from anywhere? Maybe it is the fact the loch is well cared for and the fish well fed on a rich natural diet. It might be the challenge of difficult conditions and the adapting of skills. Or is it the proximity of crystal waters with only the wind and the big sky for company? Well yes, it is all of these things and much more besides. Fishing to me is a great and continuous learning process and I echo the words of R. C. Bridgett when he said, 'the more one thinks about the sport the greater is the pleasure derived from it'. I find no greater joy in fishing than when I adapt an old tactic or try a new concept, or when I pause to discover an insect I did not know was present or simply try a cast over a different spot. Indeed, when I am teaching novice loch fishers I gain a lot of insight into my own fishing; they will ask questions I had never thought of and experiment with ideas I would not think possible. There is a deep satisfaction for me in passing my knowledge to others and there is no finer feeling than seeing the eyes light up as they catch a first trout or succeed with a new technique for the first time.

As a final source of motivation then, let me give you a few examples of what I consider classic trout lochs, waters which inspire my confidence or stretch my knowledge to the very limit. They have given me infinite pleasure in terms of angling and of panorama, indeed they are waters where that wonderful learning experience seems to go on for ever. I would emphasise I have made but a small selection of my own special places but I cite them confidently as examples of some of the really classic loch fishing accessible in Scotland.

I am inordinately lucky to live in the far north amongst some of the finest trout lochs in Britain yet every time I go angling I too have to decide a set of priorities for the day. If, for example, I am looking for a dour and difficult test of skill I have two options: the first, the nearby Reay lochs, which drive me mad but where I have seen fish as long as my arm move, or, further afield, there is always a trip to Durness in Sutherland in prospect, where the gin-clear limestone lochs offer the chance of trout equally large but no easier to extract. On both these differing yet similar waters the challenges are immense with the need to constantly revise and switch tactics between dry, wet fly or nymphs, floating or intermediate lines, sometimes all in the one morning! I love using a size 10–12 dry fly here on light tackle and floating line, something like a dry Soldier Palmer or a dry Ke He and just when the sun dips behind the hills in late evening is the witching hour as those big sulking browns edge into the shallows to feed. Ghostly shapes V the surface and fishy shadows send tingles down my spine. Either at Reay or Durness these are enigmatic, difficult waters, dour as death yet capable of producing world-class fish and they stretch my knowledge, inspire and frustrate me, and if I want to engage in taxing fishing that is where I go.

However, there are also times when I need confidence boosting and a good pace of sport. Specimen hunting is all very well but all that relentless brainstorming saps morale a bit and everybody needs some fast-moving fishing now and again. Then I have a choice of two nearby waters, either my happy hunting ground of Loch Calder, home of wet-fly teams on a floating line worked amongst superb little bays and inlets which hold dashing, spirited trout of all shapes and sizes. It is rare to have a blank here and all the fish fight superbly with Zulu, Bibio, Soldier Palmer, Ke He or Invicta doing the business. Or I might step out for a day on the Melvich hill lochs but a short puff up the hill behind my home. These are not 'expert's' waters yet they still provide a match for most angler's skills with big trout amongst the little ones. Size 10 wets are most commonly on my cast with those Kate McLarens and Zulus the most effective on floating or intermediate line; however, by mid-season a dry fly also comes into its own in both areas. Despite the bald appearance of the Melvich lochs set on a high moorland plateau they are actually remarkably fertile with mayfly and much sedge on the go. They make a delightful contrast to lowland, slightly agricultural Calder and are 'away from it all' hill lochs where the isolation is restorative and my encounters with trout always dramatic. Even if the fish are not rising the view down Strath Halladale is quite fantastic on a summer's night with the sun dropping burning gold behind the western hills.

Then again my needs may be to travel away from my comparative flat lands of limestone and marl and into some wilder scenery with big glowering hills and much more rugged backdrops. For sheer grandeur I find the Fort William/Glenfinnan area hard to beat and everywhere you look seems to be dominated by the Nevis range of hills but there is always the grand option of the Sheil and Mallaig area with the huge expanse of Loch Morar at the end of it. This is traditional wet-fly floating line country for me with the odd big fish found in amongst the brightly speckled ones, but I go there as much as for the complete change of scene as the fishing potential. Sometimes there is a need to look up at the impassive mountains and contemplate the awesome silence.

Or my priority may be an exotic 'escape' and I like to enjoy the romance of the Scottish Islands occasionally. I never know quite why the fishing is so much better after a boat trip out from the mainland but it is! I have visited the delicious lochs of Orkney several times and though the bigger lochs like Harray and Hundland claim my attentions the little loch of Clumley, sweetly clear and marl-bottomed holds some excellently conditioned trout. Another traditional 'loch-style home', but Clumley is wading only and it is all about stalking that big one with as many blanks as successes. Again it is demanding fishing and nymph and wet are used just as much as dry fly. My best fish on Clumley was on a Connemara Black and I reckoned it to be 2–3lb but success was short-lived when it headed for an old wall and dashed out the hook – such is fishing!

Finally, if I simply want lots of different types of fishings with many differing sizes of trout I almost invariably head west to the Lochinver or Scourie areas with their sweetie-shop choice of lochs. Some of those lochs around the Stoer area where McDonald Robertson and Wellington plied their rods in the 1940s and 50s are among my most favoured, gin-clear and difficult as hell but the more remote ones have some monster trout hiding in them. Of equal merit though are the numerous hill lochs bursting with smaller free-spirited fish where I can spend a day catching and returning dozens of hard-fighting trout. In these lovely areas of Sutherland it is possible to spend a day walking and fishing without seeing another soul, my only companions the eagle and the deer.

Only a few favourites then to send you on your way for I must not keep you, but before you set off on your own quest for an angling nirvana let me gently remind you that perfecting skills and visiting new waters are the tangible part of angling, there is always that wonderfully intangible aspect to consider. You might recall in the Introduction I mentioned that there was something so captivating about fishing for wild loch trout that I could never fully describe it. While I have explained tackle and techniques, the environment and the behaviour of the fish there is still that little something about wild loch fishing that truly I cannot put my finger on. It is almost a spiritual thing for when you are enjoying your angling it is there with you, and then when you leave the loch you leave it behind, until next you visit, a little piece of your soul perhaps. Fishing for wild loch trout requires ability and certain skills which can be learned from books like these, but the ultimate enjoyment of Scottish loch fishing comes from loving that tradi-tional sense of place, following in the paths of the great buccaneers of

Sometimes it is all about 'being there'.

angling, fishing in magnanimous sympathy with the environment and the conditions and above all learning all the time. No one knows everything about wild trout angling; if we did, the enticing mystique of it all would be lost, the fun is in the finding out. To me there are no bad days on the loch; some are admittedly much better than others, but the enjoyment comes as much from simply 'being there'.

When I fish for loch trout I feel privileged, lucky to be amongst nature at its finest, the loch, the hills and the sky, my constant uncritical friends. And when the first pluck and splash of a trout shakes me into gear I am reminded that if it were not for this wild fish of ours it would be unlikely I would be enjoying my country in this way at all. I urge you to remember the fact that at the heart of this pleasure is the wild brown trout and as we approach another century we must think of more of ways of conserving and nurturing this angling resource of ours, so well loved, yet often it seems forgotten in the clamour to conserve the more glamorous and potentially more lucrative salmon. All game fish are priceless to me no matter whether they migrate out to sea or live out their lives in limpid inland waters.

Go now and enjoy Scotland's wild trout lochs and I wish you as many fish to your rod as you would want though ask you take only what you really need. The loch trout has been so long a central part of Scotland's angling heritage I rather hope that, with a little help and unified co-operation from us all, whether as anglers, fishery managers or riparian owners, he will be allowed to stay that way.

Appendix I

Quick Reference Guide

Weather Conditions, Trout Diet and the Angler's Tactics

March–April: cool, unsettled, windy, sudden volatile changes in weather; take advantage of any mild dull days and fish at the warmest parts of the day between 11 a.m. and 3 p.m. Black midge usually hatch around 12 noon, stoneflies hatch in warmer conditions and fish may be full of stonefly nymphs; early olives and some small sedges appear from April on. Overwintered fish may be full of all-year fodder ('AY'*) like caddis, Coch Y Bondu beetle, snails or shrimp; some bottom-feeding fish feed exclusively on these all season. Use dark wet artificials, e.g., Zulu, Blae and Black, Pennel, Grouse and Claret on floating or intermediate line, occasional sinkers. Nymphs will work with patience.

May–June: warmer spring conditions; some difficult, very sunny hot periods but balanced with increased periods of settled weather; occasional but annoying periods of strong SE winds; increased fish and insect activity, cow dung fly from around early May; mayfly hatches on certain lime-bearing lochs in mid-June in the Highlands plus usual midge, stonefly, sedge and olive hatches and 'AY' bottom fodder; hawthorn flies appear in May, clouds of irritating caenis on limestone/more alkaline lochs late June; anglers should fish all day in dull weather or fish at either end of the day if overly bright. Use mixed artificials, e.g., Soldier Palmer, Zulu, Pennel, Invicta and those of that ilk plus more dry-fly work, e.g., dry Wickham's, French Partridge etc. Predominantly floating line.

July–August: mild, dull, wet weather a feature of July, quite settled and not too windy; fish all day in dull weather otherwise evening fishing is good after a sunny day. Profuse insect life, all species of sedge, stonefly, mayfly, midge, olives and nasty biting insects start! Daddy-long-legs appear from around mid-July. August has stickleback fry appearing but can be difficult, very midgy and often thundery, unexpected cold snaps at the month end and if it is a humid month fish may be very dour and concentrate solely on that 'AY' bottom feeding. Large red sedge profuse and red-legged bibio flies appear August. Fish early morning dull conditions if you can stand the biting 'harpies' (midges). Good mix of traditional wet or dry flies; dry Daddy, dry Bibio or Soldier Palmer very effective; floating or intermediate lines; fishing static buzzers in surface film might work but generally a lot of changing of tactics required in challenging fishing.

September through to 6 October: increased rainfall, cooler temperatures, sudden squalls, intermittent gales a noticeable feature. Spectacular core week of fishing around mid-month usually after freshening rains. All day and midday fishing the most productive while fish actively feed on stickleback, snails, caddis and any hatching insects. Freshwater snails and stickleback are particularly profuse in shallows. Trout feed hard on 'AY' fodder and any airborne terrestrials. Traditional wet fly do best with less dry used; Kate McLaren, Blue Zulu, Silver Invicta, Butcher variants etc., mainly floating line, some intermediate.

October to March (off season): heavy rain late October often hails first spawning run of browns. Mild winter encourages better survival of alevins, wet spring allows fry to return to loch. Start of season normally quite good from 15 March after mild winter. Conversely harsh winter with frosts but little rain delays the onset of spring; good early fishing can be put back and/or disrupted by torpid trout, a lack of insect hatches and slowed invertebrate activity in the loch.

---

* 'AY' is the bottom fodder for trout usually present 'all year' in most lochs but in varying quantity; shrimp only present in less acid waters. Note some, usually large, trout may feed solely off the bottom and rarely rise to the surface fly.

Appendix II

Translations of Gaelic Loch Names

Visiting anglers to the Highlands may find a little assistance in the translation of Gaelic names for lochs helpful:

Loch Beg: Little loch; refers to size of water, useful to know if you have to walk round it!

Loch nam Breac (or *nam Breac Buidhe*):   Loch of (golden) trout; any loch with *Breac* in its title almost always mean trout are present, but golden trout are normally of better size.

Loch Caol: Narrow loch, often a long, thin ribbon of water with a deep cold centre.

Loch na Caorach: Loch of the sheep, usually your only companions.

Loch a Choire: Loch in the corrie; corrie lochs can be high and infertile in a scooped basin of rock. Dramatic surroundings but fish size will vary.

Loch Clach (or *nan Clach*):   Stony lochs; this usually refers to the shoreline and wading can be tiresome struggling over boulders, but it may be worthwhile if the boulders also harbour a good variety of aquatic life for the trout to feed on.

Loch nan Clachan Geala (or *Clach Geala*):   Loch of the white stones; any loch with a white stone reference is likely to have a limestone derivative present and normally holds large well-fed trout.

Loch Crocach (or *Creagach* or similar):   Rocky or craggy loch; same interpretation as *Clach* will apply.

Loch Cuileag, Culag: Loch of the fly; could refer to insect life present, possibly the method of fishing.

Loch Dubh: Black or dark loch; normally refers to the colour of the water which can be very peat-stained and acidic, any fish are likely to be small.

Loch Eaglaise: Loch of the church; usually meant there was a church in the vicinity of the loch at one time, as Eaglaise Beg/Mor in Strath Halladale, Sutherland.

Loch an Eilein (or *Eilanach*):   The loch of islands; islands normally are good fishy areas to try, giving food and shelter to the trout.

Loch Eun (or *Uaine*):   Green loch; could be a water of rich feeding, green will refer to surroundings or water coloration.

Loch Fiadhaidh (or *Fada*):   Sometimes refers to a long loch, also means a wild loch, usually referring to its immediate surroundings.

Loch Fionn: White loch; 'fionn' can also mean cold or pale but a mention of white stone may mean limestone derivatives present, see *Clach Geala*.

Loch Gainich (or *Gainmhich* or similar):   Sandy loch; sandy lochs are difficult to judge - areas of sand can be sterile or alternatively can be alkaline glacial sands and provide rich feeding like Loch Lanlish at Durness.

Loch Garve: Rough loch, normally refers to exposed windy waters.

Loch Glas (or *Glaic* or similar):   Grey loch; not a great deal of help as a considerable number of lochs look grey from a distance.

Loch Gorm: Blue loch, as above.

Loch Meadie: Narrow loch; can also mean shallow loch.

Loch Mhuilinn: Loch of the mill; sometimes meant a corn or water mill had been situated nearby at one time.

Loch na Moine: Loch of peat; can also mean an acidic peat bog surrounds the loch; if there is no pH-adjusting limestone in the area the trout are likely to be small.

Loch Mor, Mhor or More: Big loch, self-explanatory.

Loch Poll (or *Pollain*):   Boggy loch; similar interpretation of na Moine and if wading take great care near bogs.

Loch na Seilge: Loch of the Hunter. A number of lochs in the north are called by this title; I like it as it conjures up images of stalking fish, though I suspect it refers more to deer stalking taking place in the vicinity.

Loch Sgeirach (or *Skerray* or similar):   Loch of skerries; usually productive waters with skerries providing good food and shelter for trout.

Appendix III

Useful Addresses/Organisations.

Institute of Fisheries Management (Scottish Branch), Secretary Gordon Struthers, Torshavn, Lettoch Rd, Pitlochry, PH16 5AZ.
Salmon and Trout Association, Fishmongers' Hall, London Bridge, London EC4R 9EL.
Scottish Anglers' National Association, Caledonia House, South Gyle, Edinburgh EH12 9DQ.
Scottish Stillwater Fisheries Association, Secretary Jim Boyd, 20 Kelvin Drive, Kirkintilloch, Glasgow G66 1BS.
Scottish Tourist Board, 23 Ravelston Terrace, Edinburgh EH4 3EU.

Select Bibliography

Historical References

Black Palmer *Scotch Loch Fishing* (1892)
R. C. Bridgett *Loch Fishing in Theory and Practice* (Herbert Jenkins, (1924)
Marquis of Granby *The Trout* (Fur, Feather and Fin series, 1890)
McDonald Robertson *In Scotland with a Fishing Rod* (Herbert Jenkins, 1935)
McDonald Robertson *Wade the River Drift the Loch* (Oliver & Boyd, 1948)
William Robertson MD *The Angling Resorts of Scotland* (W. Hodge & Co., 1935)
W. C. Stewart *The Practical Angler* (A. & C. Black, 1857 & other editions)
Three Anglers *How to Catch Trout* (Douglas and Foulis, 1943 – first published 1888)

Trout and Natural History

Frost & Brown *The Trout* (Collins New Naturalist Series, 1967)
John Goddard *Waterside Guide* (Collins Willow, 1991 revised edition)
Macon Worthington *Life in Lakes and Rivers* (Collins New Naturalist Series, 1974)
Maitland & Campbell *Freshwater Fishes* (Harper Collins, 1992)
Derek Mills *Salmon & Trout* (Oliver & Boyd, 1971)
H. E. Towner Coston *The Swift Trout* (Collins, 1946)

Fishing Guides/Locations

L. Crawford *Caithness & Sutherland Trout Loch Country* (North of Scotland Newspapers, 1991)
L. Crawford *An Angler's Year in Caithness & Sutherland* (Northern Times, 1992)
S. Headley *A Trout Fishing Guide to Orkney* (Headley Chaddock paperback guide © 1985)
M. Mclaren and W. B. Currie *The Fishing Waters of Scotland* (John Murray 1972)
B. Sandison *Trout Lochs of Scotland* (Harper Collins 1983)
Shetland Anglers' Association *A Guide to Shetland Trout Angling* (Shetland Isles Tourism 1994 paperback)
STB *(annual guide) Scotland for Game, Sea and Coarse Fishing* (Pastime publications)
Where to Fish (annual guide) (Harmsworth/IPC)

General Reading

J. Buckland *Pocket Guide to Trout and Salmon Flies* (Mitchell Beazley, 1986)
G. Bucknall *To Meet the First March Brown* (Swan Hill, 1994)
M. Foster *Days of Sea, Loch and River* (Michael Joseph, 1979)
C. Jardine *Dark Pools, the Dry Fly and the Nymph* (Crowood Press, 1991)
C. B. McCully *A Dictionary of Fly Fishing* (Oxford University Press paperback edition 1993)
T. Stewart *Two Hundred Popular Flies and How to Tie Them* (A & C Black paperback edition 1991)

Index